Nightlight

Nightlight

A MEMOIR

Janine Avril

alyson books
NEW YORK

MANUFACTURED IN THE UNITED STATES OF AMERICA

THIS TRADE PAPERBACK ORIGINAL IS PUBLISHED BY ALYSON BOOKS
245 WEST 17TH STREET, NEW YORK, NEW YORK 10011
DISTRIBUTION IN THE UNITED KINGDOM BY
TURNAROUND PUBLISHER SERVICES LTD.
UNIT 3, OLYMPIA TRADING ESTATE, COBURG ROAD, WOOD GREEN
LONDON N22 6TZ ENGLAND

FIRST EDITION: SEPTEMBER 2007

07 08 09 10 11 a 10 9 8 7 6 5 4 3 2 1

ISBN: 1-59350-012-1
ISBN-13: 978-1-59350-012-2

LIBRARY OF CONGRESS CATALOGING-IN-PUBLICATION DATA ARE ON FILE.

COVER DESIGN BY VICTOR MINGOVITS
INTERIOR DESIGN BY CHARLES ANNIS

To my family.
And in loving memory
of my parents.

Acknowledgments

First and foremost, I would like to thank Shannon Berning, my original editor on this project, who allowed me this amazing opportunity. Next, thank you to my second editor, Joseph Pittman, for guiding me wisely and with compassion. Thank you to everyone at Alyson Books who believed in this story. And thank you from the bottom of my heart to everyone in my life who encouraged my writing and/or assisted with the process: Amanda Insall, Ruchey Sharma, Brij and Kirin Sharma, Grace Moon, Ronnie Accordino, Angela Jimenez, Jamie Ayers, Stacey Cohen, Meredith Young, Robert Accordino, Heidi Mochari, Kierra Foster-ba, Matthew Nagin, Michelle Grove, A.L., Margaux Wexberg, Farah Miller, Terry and Jeff Greenstein, Ronda and Joel Wolf, Mai, Sara Jacobs, Geri Deluca, Robert Viscusi, Rachel Green, Joni and Tom Keating, Mikyum Kim, Laure Conklin Kamp, Michael Accordino, Lamar Herrin, Tania Katan, Romy Mancini, Jeffrey Theis, and Jeff Wald.

Author's Note

Each of the scenes of this memoir is true to the spirit of what happened. Certain names and identifying characteristics have been changed to protect privacy.

Forethought

Throughout my childhood, my mother turned on nightlights throughout our home before everyone went to sleep. They were narrow bulbs with thin lines of light. Semitransparent plastic covers surrounded them, creating gentle halos around them, only vaguely revealing that which was in a room.

A nightlight is an object of notable power. It cannot hide all the mysteries of the night, nor can it conquer all of a child's fears of what they cannot see once the room lights are shut out. Yet, it can often make the difference between falling asleep and staying awake afraid. Its soothing light is a comfort amidst what is frightening to so many children: the dark.

In the story that is to follow, I liken a nightlight to a secret. A secret is sometimes told to protect you and, in many ways, it does. It shields from you that which will make your life more painful. On the other hand, that which you don't know is still there, continually shaping your life.

Part One

Mommy

CHAPTER ONE

ONE OF MY EARLIEST MEMORIES is of my mother falling and screaming. I was four. It was 1980. We lived in a crappy rental apartment in Great Neck, New York, across the street from a small square park. In the park's wading pool there were fountains shaped like penguins that spouted water from their mouths and noses. An ice cream truck drove up and down the park's west stretch, selling Toasted Almond bars, Chocolate Eclairs, Creamsicles, Push-Ups and more. The grass was covered with dandelions—the bright yellow ones adored by bees—and the ripe ones—white and fluffy, aching for a cool breath to scatter their spores into the wind.

I had no clue that it was Mr. Rogers who voiced all of the characters of *The Neighborhood of Make Believe*. I was still filled with childlike illusions, a nursery school girl, enrolled at the Romper Room School on Lakeville Road, a windy service road off the Long Island Expressway. Mommy said that my school had nothing to do with Romper Room on channel nine, which my cousin Meredith was on. I really wished it did—fame already intrigued me.

I was friends with most of the children at school, except for this wild boy named Jason Snow, who'd once clawed my face with his fingernails during an altercation on the playground. He created a bloody diagonal line across my nose, which changed quickly into a scar. Mommy was frantic and furious when she came to pick me up at school to take me on our daily expedition of domestic errands. Fuming, she told my nursery school teacher Miss Susan that Jason Snow ought to be home-schooled as he was a menace to the other children at Romper Room.

The school was in the basement of a red-bricked church. In my young mind, the world was populated with two types of people, Christians and Jews. Thankfully, Mommy said that I could be friends with both, although it was important to remember that I was Jewish.

Mommy's name was Ilene and she was a pretty brunette. She picked me up at school one day in our beat-up two-door Le Mans, the ashtray still filled with Papa's Vantage cigarette butts. She was six months pregnant.

"I have some errands to run," she smiled at me. She always had errands to run, and I was her agreeable companion. She took me to Breyers ice cream shop off Middleneck Road to buy me a frozen chocolate-covered banana. Breyers was my favorite ice cream haunt—I liked it much better than Häagen-Dazs. The reason was that I loved the owner's daughter, Antoinette, who always gave me free multicolored sprinkles. Her father, Marty, didn't mind. I was also fond of

Marty because he looked like Mr. Rogers and once helped me cough up the piece of the pink, plastic spoon that Mommy noticed was missing as I ate from my Dixie cup. Mommy bought herself a strawberry ice cream cone. Strawberry was her favorite flavor, Rum Raisin the runner-up.

Her errands included picking up a whole chicken at the kosher butcher and returning a pair of Mary Janes that didn't fit me correctly at the Jack & Jill shoe store. Perhaps I loved Jack & Jill as passionately as Breyers ice cream due to the pretzels. They were tall, thin, crispy sticks, coated with salt. I liked to lick them until all the salt had dissolved into my mouth, the pretzel soggy, waiting to be chewed, savored, and made to last. Sometimes the cashier offered me two from the glass jar next to the register—if Mommy said it was okay that day, not too close to dinner time.

She turned off of Grace Avenue onto Barstow Road and into the parking lot of our building. Our spot had a large, yellow seven painted across it on the black tar pavement. Mommy took the bags out of the trunk as I trailed behind her into the building's back entrance, through a heavy brown door with brass handles and a diamond-shaped window. The parking lot overlooked Grace Avenue Park, where I spent much time with her, picking those ripe white dandelions to blow into the wind, running through the penguin sprinklers, soaking in the wading pool in my bikini when the air was warm enough, demanding ice cream each time the truck swung by, playing its same song.

The building's elevator was out of order; a sign was

lazily pasted across its leathery, cushioned door. We'd have to take the stairs again, which we used the few times that the building caught fire, arousing my very earliest feelings of terror. Those fires were quickly extinguished, but our escapes out of the building to wait in the park were nerve-racking nonetheless.

It was three flights to the fourth floor where we lived. We'd made it up only one flight when Mommy fell to the gray, cement floor of the stairwell, screaming and clutching her right ankle. She rocked it on her lap, bending her body forward and lowering her head. I sat next to her, paralyzed, unsure of how to help as her cries echoed through the empty stairwell. I thought of running for Terry, my best friend Jamie's mother, but I didn't want to leave Mommy alone. Papa wasn't home; he was working at a restaurant in Manhattan, and he always came home late, way past my bedtime.

Her high-pitched screams haunted me. She screamed like that every time she twisted her foot, a common occurrence that seemed to come out of nowhere, and each time, I prayed to God that this would never happen again, especially not without Papa there to help.

I just couldn't help her, couldn't predict the next occurrence of her falling. All I could do when she fell was sit at her side until the pain stopped, wait for the incident to lose its color, to fade into memory.

CHAPTER TWO

PAPA DROVE THE LE MANS, Mommy occupied the passenger seat with little Luc in her arms, and I straddled the hand rest in the middle of the backseat. The car was finally cooling off. When we'd approached it in the parking lot, the door handles were like pan handles on the stove, and the blue leather of the back seat scorched my legs so badly that Mommy gave me a towel from the beach bag to sit on. But now the air conditioner was on full blast, and I had stopped my whining.

I was wearing clear jellies—the once-popular water-proof plastic sandals. On the seat next to me were our beach bags, stocked with vibrantly colored, giant beach towels from the linen closet, Papa's dark suntan oil, and a picnic lunch of leftovers—chicken parmigiana sandwiches from dinner the evening before, potato chips, and a tall can of grape-flavored Juicy Juice.

I just couldn't wait to get to the Parkwood Pool on Steamboat Road, one of Great Neck's free public pools.

After we parked, Mommy flashed our membership cards at the security checkpoint, Luc still in her arms, and Papa gave me a piggyback ride. I always felt safer riding piggyback than when he put me up on his shoulders, though being on his shoulders was thrilling . . . I saw more of the world from up there.

We staked out our territory with three lounge chairs.

Two we put in the sun but made sure one was shaded by the trees for Mommy, who didn't tolerate sun that well with her fair skin. Papa's skin was olive: he tanned easily and rarely burned.

After we'd been settled for a while, Mommy brought me to the kiddie pool where I kept my jellies on in the water. We then visited the play area. She jumped around on the hopscotch courts in the rink and rented me a hula hoop, giggling at me as I rattled it around my small body, trying to get it to stay up around my hips; it always fell to the floor within seconds. After laughing at me, she tried it herself. She was, of course much, better at it than I was and I admired her for that.

Papa passed Luc to her when we returned, saying he wanted to sleep. Completely ignoring his pleas, I crawled onto his back, oily from his suntan lotion, and shook him.

"Let me sleep, doll," he said sweetly—he loved to sleep in the sun. Unlike me or Mommy, he could fall asleep no matter how hot it was. I lay on his back for a while and tried to sleep myself but couldn't, the skin on my face getting greasy, smelling of coconuts.

I nudged him again. "Papa, take me to the diving board." He played dead for only a couple more seconds before he conceded.

"Okay. Okay, already!"

The adult pool was the challenge, the place where I felt grown up. Papa dove head first into the pool and swam below the larger of the two diving boards—the smaller one was only several feet high.

I climbed the high board and slowly tiptoed across, thinking of Wendy walking the plank in *Peter Pan*. It always looked easier to jump from the ground, and I started to lose my nerve when I finally got up there. Papa was in the water, waiting for me and cheering me on.

"Okay, doll, jump!" he encouraged. "Jump!"

Trusting him enough, I held my nose and leaped feet first, straight into his arms, there to catch me, to swim alongside me to the metallic ladder of the deep end.

"Did you have fun?" Mommy smiled when we returned, her chair inclined in the shade, an open book of Robert Frost's poetry on her lap. Luc was asleep at her side. I nodded and smiled, still excited from the rush of jumping from the high board. Papa made me laugh by falling onto his lounge chair, face forward, playing dead again.

We had a ritual. After Parkwood, we went to this nearby track. Papa was the runner among us although he wasn't running in marathons yet. Those days he just ran the track as Mommy, Luc, and I watched from the bleachers. When he finished he would take me on the enchanted trail while Mommy waited with Luc. He discovered the entrance to the trail at a crossing in the woods behind the track, and I assumed that it was top secret, that only we knew about it. The woods were a labyrinth, offering many directions in which to go. I thought Papa was so smart for knowing which way to head each time there was a fork in the trail. No matter how complicated it seemed, he always managed to get us back out, back to Mommy and Luc, and I marveled at him for finding the way. I trusted his judgment. He still had the power of a mythical god . . . all knowing and protective.

CHAPTER THREE

TROUBLING EVENTS repeated themselves: my mother screaming when she fell. My father coming home from work at nearly daybreak with some odd excuse.

It was 1983; I was six and three quarters. I awoke in the dark, startled, on my Sesame Street sheets. I had taken my nightgown off in my sleep. Luc was less than four feet away from me, his blue plastic crib parallel to my single bed. A peach-colored nightlight was in the socket next to his crib, illuminating him enough so that I could see the silhouette of his tiny body. There were nightlights turned on throughout the apartment. They created a faint glow over the darkness.

I had a feeling that Mommy was still awake, alone in bed. I hated to wake up and think this, and was always relieved when I'd peek through the door of the master bedroom and see my parents sleeping together, Papa snoring, Mommy resting quietly. For a stretch of time back then it was a crapshoot—whether he'd be there or not. I would often be distraught after walking to their room to find him missing, yet again.

Naked, I wrapped my Ernie and Bert sheet around me like a long dress and braved my way down the creaky wooden hallway of the apartment toward their room. One nightlight was lit in the hallway; a stronger glow emanated from the door of their bedroom.

I knocked but didn't wait for a response before opening the door. Mommy was sitting upright in bed, wearing her rose-colored robe with the "I" for Ilene monogrammed onto the right breast pocket. The portable black-and-white television set mounted on the bureau inaudibly played a rerun of *Laverne & Shirley*. A crossword puzzle was on her lap. She spotted me.

"You're up?" she asked, despite the obvious. "How long have you been awake?"

"I just woke up. Where's Papa?"

She sighed. "He's going to be very late, honey." Looking at the red lights of the digital clock on the night table, I saw that it was four a.m.

"Where is he?" I pressed and Mommy paused.

"He fell asleep on the Long Island railroad accidentally on his way home from work earlier. The train went all the way back to the city and he has to catch a new train back."

Fell asleep on the Long Island railroad . . . I'd been on the LIRR when Grandpa Levy, Mommy's father, escorted me on a day trip to the Museum of Natural History to show me the dinosaur exhibit. On the train ride, people could watch the subtle shift as they left suburbia and entered New York City. Lush, green trees morphed into faded, tired buildings.

Once inside the tunnel, the box car lights flickered, going off entirely sometimes. A family of four—our little family for instance—could occupy a whole row of seats together.

I pictured Papa asleep on the train, missing the conductor's cues, so unconscious that the words "Great Neck! Now arriving in Great Neck!" never registered in his brain.

"Can I stay in here with you?" I asked Mommy. "Until he comes home?"

"Yes, but you need to try to get to sleep. You can't wait up for him."

"Okay," I said, crawling under the pine-green comforter, which contrasted warmly with the room's beige walls and carpeting.

"Are you scared?" I asked her.

"No," she said softly. "I'm not scared." She played with my long, fine brown hair, which she had combed carefully with No More Tangles—in spite of my protests—before I went to bed, after washing my hair in the bath with Johnson's baby shampoo. This was our nightly ritual, and I always hated having my hair combed after the bath because it got so many knots.

"I feel better now that he called and I know he's alright," she added.

My young body occupying only a small portion of Papa's half of the bed, I turned on my side to face Mommy. When I held my hand out to her, she grasped it in her lap. My next conscious moment was of Papa lifting me carefully into his arms, his beer breath on my face, his shirt reeking of cigarettes. I pretended to still be asleep as he carried me drunkenly down the hallway to my bed, Mommy following. She gently put me back in my nightgown as I continued to feign sleep.

I waited several moments until I heard the master bedroom door close firmly, climbing back out over my bedrail, down the dimly lit hallway, eavesdropping at their door.

"Bastard. You have unbelievable fucking gall to do this to me again."

"Ilene," Papa drawled, "I'm telling you the truth."

"Well, I don't believe you. I want to know where you really were."

"Ilene. I told you. I was on the goddamned train. Jacques came by after work. We had some drinks, one too many perhaps, and I passed out."

There was a very long pause.

"*Bums* fall asleep on the train, Remy. Respectable husbands don't."

"So that's what you're calling me now? A bum?"

"That's what you are."

"Shut up."

"How many times do I have to plead for a simple, fucking phone call at a reasonable hour? Just to know where you are."

"Shut up already, will you. I want to go to sleep."

"Sleep on the couch then."

"This is my bed too. I'll sleep in it if I want."

"Fine, I'll go," Mommy snapped.

I moved from the doorway, but too late. She got to the door and saw me standing there in the glow of the night-light.

"Honey," she said regretfully. She picked me up from the floor, wiping the tears from my cheeks.

"Everything's okay. Everything's okay." She held me closely, clutching me against her.

Papa walked out from the bedroom. "It was just a fight, doll. We didn't mean anything."

I looked at Mommy for confirmation of his words.

She nodded. "We just got angry, but it didn't mean anything. We love each other very much. People get angry at each other, but they still love each other."

I nodded, but I didn't know if I believed them. I know that I wanted to. . . .

"Will you go to sleep now then, together, in your room?"

"Yes," Mommy said firmly.

"Yes," Papa agreed.

They tucked me back into bed.

"*Je t'aime, Kiki*," Papa said.

"I love you," Mommy said, kissing me on the forehead for the third time that night. "Goodnight. Don't let the bed bugs bite." She left me in the room, across from Luc and the peach-colored nightlight. I drifted back to sleep.

Papa's excuses for why he didn't come home on time always seemed bizarre, but never were completely implausible. Once, he said he had been held at knifepoint at work by some Mafiosos for refusing to comply with their sanitation requirements. He told us that he was held hostage in the basement of the restaurant until he agreed to give in to their demands. This was meant to explain his arrival home at nearly six a.m.

Sometimes Mommy would be on the phone with Grandma and Grandpa, frantic. Other times she would just seethe at him alone. If I woke up and felt afraid, she didn't want me to worry, but I could never help it. Her assurances didn't really succeed in calming me. I worried about him. I worried that he'd crashed his car drunk because he drove that way. I had an incredible sense of relief to see him home eventually no matter how angry he made me or Mommy by pulling one of his late-night stunts.

CHAPTER FOUR

LE RELAIS ON MADISON AVENUE in Manhattan was the restaurant Papa worked at in the late 1970s and early 1980s after working as head chef at the Stork Club on East Fifty-third Street.

I look back on those sweet days that he took me to that restaurant, perhaps to give my mother a break along with the fact that I liked to go. For him, it was just a day at work. For me, it was a joyous occasion, from the moment he strapped me in with the seat belt in the old, blue Le Mans, to the moment we arrived home in the parking lot on Barstow Road, into our spot with the faded yellow seven.

I felt curious, admiring eyes upon me from the first instant of making my way in through the stained glass French doors of the restaurant, holding Papa's hand, basking in the warm smiles of the maitre d' and the waiters.

Papa was head chef, responsible for making the French cuisine spectacular. I accompanied him as he changed out of his slick, black leather jacket and ripped jeans into his bright white, freshly pressed chef uniform. I went with him into the walk-in freezers, which he promised we could never get locked into; still I was afraid. He gave me a fresh, green plastic carton of strawberries to wash and eat.

He taught me what each of the different forks and knives in the table settings were for and showed me how a cloth napkin, which seemed at first to be a boring rectangular piece of fabric, could be folded like origami into a voluptuous flower. At the staff lunch, he served me steak and eggs.

"Very French," he laughed to everyone. "My daughter likes French food, but she's really very American." He stuck his tongue out at me and winked. He loved to tease me by calling me very American—he knew it got my goat.

I was only allowed to stay in the kitchen with him through part of his very long shift. The kitchen was too hot for a delicate little girl. So instead, I sat in the dining room with the bag of activities Mommy packed for me: my favorite game (Memory), my paper dolls, and my jigsaw puzzle of the United States. I would wander back into the kitchen every once in a while to see Papa, mesmerized by the sight of him. He acted as if he was on stage in the costume of his all white chef gown, sandwiched between two gigantic stoves covered with copper pans above blue and orange flames and filled with sauces: some light, some dark, most thick and heavy. The air smelled of garlic, onions, olive oil, meat, fish, poultry, vegetables, all mixed together in a mouth-watering aroma. Papa, as he was in any restaurant I'd ever seen him in, was running the show, completely absorbed in the sensations of his culinary art.

CHAPTER FIVE

A PORTAL OPENED for Papa in his adulthood, well after he married Mommy and became a father to me and Luc. He first discovered his true identity at the age of thirty-five, which shook the foundations of who he thought he was, sending him on a vital journey of self-discovery.

He was raised in a tiny town in the French Loire Valley region called Font D'Vreau, the son of a beautiful woman named Jeanne and a man named Pierre. Pierre was a lowly jail warden, but still the patriarch of the Avril family—a poor and downtrodden group. The great trauma of my father's youth was when Jeanne abandoned him and his five siblings to work as a maid for a wealthy man named Henri. Jeanne took care of Henri's children while her own were left motherless and though they kept contact with her mother for a while, each of the siblings, and Papa, eventually cast her off. My father was the only child who ever really forgave

Jeanne. Mommy encouraged him to make peace with her mother when they got engaged. She couldn't understand how any man could refuse to speak to his mother, no matter what bad things she had done.

When Papa was thirty-five, Henri's oldest daughter Isabelle contacted him. She told him that she was his half sister. Isabelle overheard a conversation between her parents. Jeanne, the maid who'd practically raised her as a child, had once become impregnated by her father and had a son named Remy. Astonished by the news, she tracked down Jeanne and then my father in America, wanting to connect with her half brother.

Isabelle's call shifted Papa's perception of his life. When his mother went to work for Henri, leaving her own children behind, she had abandoned him for the man who was his father. A light bulb went off in his brain about why some of the townspeople had called him a "bastard" when he was a boy. He was the bastard son of Jeanne and Henri. He had known that townspeople had thought his mother was a whore who slept around outside her marriage, but he didn't know that he was the one illegitimate child of the Avril kids.

Mommy, Luc, and I accompanied Papa back to France to meet Henri when I was eight years old. It was our third family trip overseas to visit Papa's homeland since I was born. Papa never got over his nostalgia for France, and we traveled there quite frequently.

Unlike the Avrils, many of whom lived in government housing or small, cramped quarters, Henri's house was impressive, built on a large plot of land. I remember that he and Papa took a walk on the land. Luc played with Isabelle's children as Karina, Henri's wife, prepared lunch. I remember Karina being a friendly person while it is curious that she would have been accepting of a child that her husband had from an extramarital affair. Mommy and I sat on a balcony which overlooked the land, drinking Orangina.

"This is a really important day for Papa," she explained to me, using the voice she used when she was about to tell me something shocking. It was troubling to learn that Henri was my real relative. All of those nights we'd spent before at Pierre, the jail warden's house, I'd believed that he was my grandfather. To learn that he was not related to me by blood was unsettling and obviously even more unsettling for Papa who had so many questions and a deep need to know the man to whom he was biologically tied. While Henri had never sought out a relationship with Papa as a child, since that would have been too scandalous for both his family and Jeanne's, he welcomed him as an adult.

CHAPTER SIX

MOMMY'S LIFE began two years before Papa's, across the Atlantic Ocean in Queens, New York. Her parents, the Levys, were American-born Jews, both with lineages tracing back to anti-Semitic Russia.

The Levys were not a family of scandalous secrets like

the Avrils. However, they were a family with both sad and extraordinary stories. Those in Grandpa's family who stayed in Poland and Russia were destroyed by the Nazis. Both of Grandma's parents died from cancer before she was twenty-one-years old, leaving her an orphan under the care of her sister Sylvia and Sylvia's husband Simon Schwartz.

Grandma met Grandpa at a Valentine's Day dance in February of 1941. In March of 1941, Grandpa was drafted, sent to train for the war that broke out in December of '41. He was then sent to France to fight the Germans. But between them was a powerful and indissoluble love. They wrote to each other for over four years and got engaged on one of Grandpa's short leaves home, determined to spend their lives together.

Grandpa narrowly escaped death on Christmas Day of 1944 when he switched a work shift with a close friend to sit guard in a tanker. His friend, a solider named Johnnie Kisner, was blown to bits by an explosion during a German artillery attack on the tanker. Grandpa felt guilty while blessed to still have his life. He came home a war hero at the end of World War Two. His troops were among the first to liberate a Nazi concentration camp called Ohrdruf. He returned with all of his limbs intact, a Purple Heart, and a frozen toe, to which sensation never returned.

Relatively speaking, the troubles of Mommy's youth in Queens paled in comparison to Papa's in Font D'Vreau. She never went hungry and was never abandoned. She was never teased without understanding the nature of why she was being picked on.

I know she struggled to assert her individuality in the face of Grandma and Grandpa's overprotectiveness. Their natures were to meddle in every aspect of her life and there came a point that she needed some space . . . even if that space was temporary.

Her timing in leaving Queens to start a life thousands of miles from home was synchronized with Papa's. She wanted self reliance. She had an adventurous spirit then, and was thirsty for life's mysteries and passions. At twenty-two, following her graduation from Ithaca College, she found her way to San Francisco, landing a job and a roommate through the local PennySaver.

She dreamed of love. She wrote about it in her diaries. She was a very sentimental person, who collected many books of love poetry. She also wrote stories during the day at her secretarial jobs, yet never tried to publish them.

CHAPTER SEVEN

MOMMY WAS INVOLVED in an upsetting incident before she met Papa in 1974. Her car was parked in the garage of the building where she worked. One evening on her way back to the car, shortly after nightfall, she was grabbed by a man who tried to attack her. At the moment he tried to force her into his car, a group of people walked into the garage and her attacker ran off. After that, she felt afraid in San Francisco and contemplated coming back to the East Coast. Grandma and Grandpa wanted her to. But she tried to be brave and not dwell too much on her near abduction and what might have become of her had those people not arrived at that moment. It was shortly after that incident that she met Papa and their romance began, full swing.

He spotted her in a tavern in North Beach in 1972. He was living in the Castro, she near the Marina. He had been in the States for two years by then. He'd followed a girl he fell in love with in Paris all the way to Mexico, only to be rejected by her family who thought he was not wealthy or educated enough to marry their daughter. Heartbroken, he made his way up to Tijuana, across the American border up through California, and landed in San Francisco where he was homeless for a while. At first he slept in Golden Gate Park in a sleeping bag under the stars, waking to the morning fog. After some time, he landed a paper route job. There were certain street corners in the city where papers sold best, and, since he had no home, he slept on those corners so that he could be the first one to claim the spot in the morning to sell papers. He soon saved enough money from his paper route to get a room at the YMCA.

His only previous experience working in restaurants was as a dishwasher in Paris, where he had gone to live on his own when he was only fourteen years old. He watched the chefs he worked with carefully, and he learned a great deal about cooking, enough to talk his way into jobs with French restaurant owners in San Francisco, impressing them with his natural ability in the kitchen.

He married a woman named Theresa at some point in order to get a Green Card. It's not clear to me whether she was a lover or a friend or whether he compensated her in some way for their sham marriage, but for me, finding out that my father had a wife before my mother was similar to finding out that Pierre Avril was not my biological grandfather. I learned about it when a French cousin of mine on one of our family trips to Europe showed me the wedding invitation that my father and Theresa sent to his French family. She enjoyed shocking me with that bit of news. When I confronted my parents about it, they admitted it was the truth.

Mommy was playing pool with a girlfriend when Papa became intrigued by her simple, natural beauty . . . a brunette several shades lighter than Jeanne, eyes the color of coffee beans, a small-framed body with a flawlessly sculpted, delicately featured face.

He approached her, handed her a beer, and asked her for the next game of pool. The friend she was with became nameless, faded off into the evening with another strange man, like smoke in the bar room.

"Will you go to Lake Tahoe with me this weekend?" he asked her as the evening progressed.

"Are you crazy?" Mommy laughed. "I wouldn't go off for the weekend with a total stranger."

But she was charmed by his passion for living and his

French accent. He was different, worlds away from the Jewish doctor or lawyer that Grandma and Grandpa and other Jewish parents from Queens, New York, had in mind.

Mommy was as pretty as Papa was handsome, but she didn't know it. She didn't move through the world with the same kind of ego. His confident persona allured her while her stability, her even keel, at least in comparison to his dramatic ups and downs, drew him to her. She was "solid" he told me once. "Right to be the mother of my children."

CHAPTER EIGHT

MOMMY WANTED Grandma and Grandpa to accept Papa. She had been dating him in San Francisco for a matter of months when she called them in New York.

"This is serious. I want you to fly out here to meet him." It was the first time they received an urgent phone call like this. She was twenty-seven and getting restless to settle down and have her babies.

Grandpa and Grandma booked a weekend trip and flew out to California to meet her prospective husband.

"The minute I saw them walk into the hotel lobby together, I thought they were well matched," Grandpa said. "Then when your Papa told me he was drinking Haig & Haig, Pinch, I knew he was a classy guy. He came from poverty, but he had class nonetheless. For someone who was born into nothing and raised himself up through his own will, he was very sophisticated. He wasn't Jewish, but we could tell that he was very ambitious."

"And he was charming," Grandma contributed.

"I sensed he'd make a good living. I had confidence in him," Grandpa put in.

"And he said he'd convert. He took Hebrew lessons. A mikvah bath. He became a Jew," Grandma pointed out.

"What more could we have asked for?" Grandpa asked.

Mommy and Papa had a Jewish wedding in 1974 at a country club in Oceanside, Long Island. Papa was the sole member of his family there. The pictures, filled with innocent beaming smiles, show a twenty-four-year-old boy in a gorgeous tuxedo, marrying an elegant bride. This was the start of their life on the East Coast of America together, Grandma and Grandpa close by in the shadows to look out for them.

Grandpa was not rich but he was financially comfortable and very generous. My Uncle Benjamin, Mommy's brother, was just launching his career, yet offered Papa some money he'd saved. With the help of Grandpa, Uncle Benjamin, and Grandma's brother-in-law, Simon Schwartz, Papa gathered the funds to open a restaurant in Manhattan. In 1983, he took over a restaurant called *La Vie*, which became a fast success.

"And he made a go of it," Grandpa said, his voice getting weepy. "He made a go of it."

CHAPTER NINE

WE HAD ALREADY MOVED from the shoddy rental apartment in Great Neck to our sparkly, spacious split-level house in Roslyn Estates, Long Island, when Papa left us for a while for a reason that was not explained. I always guessed that he left because my parents argued too much.

He packed his suitcase and said goodbye to me on the latter part of the horrendous afternoon of the failed attempt to see *Oliver* on Broadway. Mommy had arranged for tickets to the show months prior but hadn't become aware that the show was canceled, moved off Broadway due to low ticket sales. Not enough people were compelled by the tragic tale of orphan Oliver Twist to keep the show afloat. I was let down. For weeks in preparation, I'd listened to the record with Mommy in the playroom, waiting for the thrill of seeing it on stage. I can distinctly hear her melodious voice in my mind and my own child soprano voice chorusing with her. *Who will buy this wonderful morning? Such a sky you never did see! Who will tie it up with a ribbon and put it in a box for me?*

Because my voice was so high pitched, I was never allowed to sing alto with the East Hills Elementary school chorus. I was jealous of the altos . . . simply because I was a soprano. If I'd been an alto, I'm sure I would have been equally as jealous of the sopranos and tried to do whatever I could do to figure out how to be one!

Mommy and I often sang to records in the playroom, or

in the car on the way to the Hofstra pool where she did her laps in the afternoons. I think I was the only audience for her wonderful singing. There was a shyness and modesty about her that would have prevented her from belting out Carly Simon's "Coming Around Again," in front of anyone but her unassuming eight year old.

There was friction the morning we drove from Roslyn to New York City to see *Oliver.* The shit only royally hit the fan when we arrived at the boarded-up, abandoned theater, not a soul waiting on line. Mommy questioned what the hell was going on. Papa assumed the manly role of finding out. Our failed plans thickened the air. I remember Mommy asking Papa what we should do now, as if the Big Apple didn't offer a plethora of engaging options. It felt as if we'd hit rock bottom.

We were walking aimlessly around the theater district, the air of doomsday upon us, when suddenly I saw one of those rides that now make me sick to watch but at the time were the most glamorous thing next to Madonna and teeny-bopper magazines. The ride was a metallic swing that swayed high into the air on both sides once turned on by the controller man. If you threw up or got thrown up on, well, it sucked for you.

Mommy opposed my going on but I begged mercilessly to go. Papa, boss man, eventually overrode her, saying I could go, either to stop my whining or to spite my mother or a lovely combination of both. Mommy tugged my arm to keep me off the ride, shrieking at Papa on the street, making such a scene that we left the scene, even though, in fact, we *were* the scene.

Upon the sad realization that it would be impossible to let things blow over and have a nice day together in the city, Mommy and Papa decided to take me home. When we arrived back in Roslyn, I was sent to watch television, very grateful for the *Little House on the Prairie* rerun. I knew every episode and could recite most of Laura Ingalls Wilder's lines. It was the episode where Mary Ingalls's baby died in the blind school that burned down. I had a disturbing draw toward melodramatic television, enraptured by tragedy at a young age. While sad episodes disturbed me, I always watched them. I was compelled by sad stories and seemed to welcome getting melancholy.

I wished Luc was home to keep me company, but he was at Grandma and Grandpa's apartment in Forest Hills. Mommy thought *Oliver* would be too advanced for him to enjoy at the age of four, since rumor had it that Fagin on Broadway was a terrifying man.

I was on the couch in the playroom with the toy chest that Papa built us, a room stocked with games and movies that overlooked our backyard basketball court, when Papa came to say goodbye. He took me fervently into his arms.

"I'll be back very soon, doll."

"Where are you going?"

"I'm not sure yet."

When I was older, I learned that Papa was gone for three weeks . . . only three weeks. At the time it felt more like three months, but I think when you're a child, twenty minutes can seem like eternity.

"Are you getting a divorce?" I asked Mommy when he drove away.

"I don't know. No. I don't know."

Papa visited me and Luc on Saturdays during the weeks that he and Mommy were separated. He stayed at his business partner François's apartment in Manhattan, close to the restaurant.

When his car arrived in the driveway, Mommy sent us outside without coming out to say hello to him. When he dropped us off at night, having eaten junk food not normally permitted and watched R-rated movies never typically allowed, he sat with us for a long time on the large rock in front of the house. He cried and told us how hard this was for him and how much he missed us and how he would spend the whole week waiting to see us again.

"Why can't you come back home?" I asked.

"Mommy has to say that it's okay."

"I'll tell her to say it's okay," I said, conviction in my voice.

"You can try," Papa said. His wide aquamarine eyes were hopeful.

From my vantage point, Mommy was mean for not letting him back, even if he bullied me sometimes and let Luc off the hook much more readily. Papa only got angry at Luc when he wouldn't finish his plate, since in our house, because people were starving in various places of the world, everyone had to finish his/her plate. And while Luc got sent to his room for not finishing his plate or had to sit at the table until he finished every iota of food, even if it was until ten o'clock at night, Papa's cruelty to me took different forms. It was my comments that did me in rather than the boycotting of dinner. The things I'd say infuriated him.

"If I don't finish my plate, people will *still* be starving."

Papa would smash my fingers with the top part of his dinner knife at such back-talking, making my knuckles sore throughout the next day.

While perhaps he had motives that as a child I could not comprehend, he did certain things that made my life miserable, things that I thought were unnecessary. Even in retrospect, I feel this.

For a period of time, he controlled what I wore to school every day. He did not want me to dress like the other kids in the neighborhood dressed.

"You will not be a Jewish American Princess. I will not let you be one," he drummed in. "Not when I grew up wearing rags and carrying coal on my back to heat my house."

His wardrobe selections served to do more than shield me from becoming a Jewish American Princess; rather, his choices caused my peers to totally ostracize me. I headed to school every day dressed like a little French girl from the 1950s, wearing frilly shirts, skirts, and loafers instead of the hip Champion sweatshirts with leggings and Converse sneakers that other kids wore. For a while, my only compatriot on the playground was a girl from the projects near the

Roslyn train tracks. Her name was Lucy Taveras and she also wore what the Roslyn school girls considered loser clothing because it was not brand name. I had become an object of ridicule among the snobbish tyrants at school.

One day, I hid a sweat suit in my book bag and changed into it on the back of the school bus before I got to school. I thought I'd make it through the day home free but Papa came home from work early and saw me without my French girl outfit on as I walked home from the bus stop. He cornered me between the washer and dryer when I walked into the house, kicking me until I promised that I would never defy his orders again. I screamed and shielded my face with my hands as Mommy tugged him, begging him to stop, as she did each time he came after me. After that, something changed. He eased up on me. I stopped playing sick at recess and hiding in the nurse's office rather than facing the rejection of girls walking away from me in the school yard. And a real hypocrite, I dropped Lucy Taveras when I finally made other friends who were *cool*.

When Papa was behaving himself, I always hoped we were at the beginning of something new. I had this undying optimism that he would finally change and stop hurting me. That childlike hope made me resent my mother's rejection of him. Her not giving him a chance was worse than his temper . . . more painful than the darkness in him that made him hurt people. She needed to give him more chances. She needed to keep trying. . . .

CHAPTER TEN

I WAS EIGHT YEARS OLD when I attended my parents so-called "second wedding." I was confused about why they were having a second wedding, when they had never ended their first marriage while aware to some degree that this show of good intentions was to counteract that which had been bad in our lives.

"Kids!" Mommy called through the secret passageway. . . . Luc had made the discovery that there was an air tunnel that led from a vent in my parents's closet to a vent in the playroom three floors below. This discovery was made when he heard Mommy and Papa talking in their closet about where to hide the safe that contained emergency cash, our birth certificates, passports, and other important family documents. Papa told Mommy to put the safe in the crawl space behind the towel shelf of the linen closet. Mommy advised me to never actually *crawl* into that crawl space . . . it was not meant for crawling. She claimed, giggling as she told me, that I could fall into the air shafts, right through the house and be lost forever. She also warned me with a more straight face never to press what was called THE PANIC BUTTON: a rectangular red button near a socket on her side of the bed that linked directly to the Roslyn police station. I teased her at first. I playfully tested her patience by putting my fingers right up to that panic button, tapping it softly enough not to set it off. The day inevitably came where I pushed the button harder than I intended to push it. Mommy could barely hear the policeman ask her for our "secret password"—San Francisco—when he called. She was as angry as she ever got when I pressed the button while Papa was at work, telling him when he arrived home from the city that she wanted my head on a silver platter.

"Kids!"

Luc was playing with his electric train set. I was choreographing a dance to Madonna's song "*Borderline*," my small, purple plastic boom box playing the cassette that was my favorite in the world. Madonna was everything to me, which is why Papa, despite Mommy's firm disapproval, took me to see *The Virgin Tour*, not covering my innocent eyes when Madonna stripped to her bra and panties on stage.

"Kids! Come upstairs and start getting ready!"

I questioned Mommy about why she and Papa were getting married when they already were. Her response was that they simply were renewing their marriage vows. I didn't understand why vows that didn't need to be renewed were being renewed.

"None of my friends's parents have renewed their vows!" I told her.

"So think about how lucky you are," she replied. "Most of your friends will never get to see their own parents married, but you and Luc will!"

Mommy's logic didn't particularly convince me. I was not easily convinced. The more I grew into myself, the more I found this to be true.

Luc took his bath first in the creamsicle-colored bathroom that we shared. After my shower when I was dressed, I found my way into my parents's room. Papa was shaving in the bathroom with the door open, a towel around his waist. Mommy sat with Luc in front of the full length mirror in her bathrobe. She put on his tie which identically matched the tie that Papa would wear. When she finished fixing him up, she motioned me over, sat me down in front of the mirror and braided my hair, holding the braids at the end with colored plastic animal barrettes.

Luc was being a pest again. He stuck his tongue out at the mirror, making silly faces to entertain himself.

"Idiot," I laughed.

"Didn't I tell you not to call your brother names?" Papa chided from the bathroom, mouth full of toothpaste. I was also not allowed to hit Luc on his back since I had the tendency to swing at him there, forcing him into odd positions.

"He'll stay in one of those positions one day. I know someone that happened to," Papa joked.

"You look very pretty and Luc you look very handsome. You will be my special guests tonight—my most distinguished guests of honor," Mommy declared.

"How many people are coming?" I asked.

"Just Grandma, Grandpa, Uncle Benjamin, and Aunt Karen. Plus François will be there at the restaurant to help out with a few other people."

"That's a lot less people than you had at your first wedding."

"Yes," Mommy agreed, "We had around a hundred people at our first wedding."

"Are you having less people at this wedding because it's less important?"

"It's not less important honey. It's just different. . . ."

I was proud of our well-dressed family as we walked out of the house that was so new to us there were still unpacked boxes everywhere. We'd lived there for only a few months, but it would take many more months to figure out the right place for everything and to furnish the rooms that were empty. In fact, it would take years for my parents to decorate the house just to their liking. Several of our apartments from Great Neck could fit into this new house at the end of a dead end street with a pool on the manicured lawn and a perfect swing set that Papa built for me and Luc in the backyard. There was so much space and no cockroaches anywhere— no need for Roach Motels. I had my own large room, a sign up on the door that Grandma Levy bought me at the Roosevelt Field flea market that said, THIS IS MY ROOM SO SCRAM! GET LOST! I could finally lock little Luc out with just a short twist of the brass lock. Mommy and Papa didn't like it when I locked him out and he came crying to them complaining, crybaby that he was, but I locked him out anyway, especially if he was being a pest.

Papa pulled the Mercedes out of our long driveway that led out to our circuitous suburban neighborhood, gated in only by looming trees. Papa, in his fancy suit, drove down Hickory Hill. He made a right onto the Serpentine and another right on the Intervale to get to the Mobil station. After filling up, he drove to the Long Island Expressway, passing the strip of ritzy shops called The Miracle Mile.

He smiled at Mommy as he drove with his left hand. With his right hand he played with her hair, squeezing his hand around her neck as a sign of endearment.

"Stop!" she laughed. He patted her thigh with his hand; I eyed them from the backseat.

"Mommy," Luc asked, "do bears sleep at night?"

"I'm sure that some bears sleep at night, Luc," she said, turning her head to see him, a look of amusement on her face.

"Don't sit on that divider like that," she scolded. Luc moved off of the hand rest, onto the right side of the backseat.

"Goddamn LIE," Papa spat. He was never one for traffic.

"We'll get there," Mommy said. "Be patient." Papa lit a cigarette.

"Must you smoke in the car, Remy?"

"I'm frustrated."

She shrugged, looked to the backseat to check up on us.

"How are you two back there?"

Luc and I got terribly bored in the traffic. We played the story game where I said one sentence and Luc said another and I said another and soon we had a silly story.

"Fine."

"How about some music?" Papa asked.

"Not CD 101.9," I insisted. He laughed.

"What kind of music then, doll, if you don't want jazz?"

"The Stones."

"Eight years old and a Rolling Stones fan. That's my girl." He searched around for a cassette, playing his favorite: *Wild Horses*.

"Everybody has to sing," Papa said. Papa liked to sing as much as Mommy did and I can also hear his voice in my mind, saying that he loved living because it was easy to do.

Papa kissed Mommy at a traffic light on Second Avenue, shortly after we drove off of the Queensboro Bridge. He headed downtown several blocks to *La Vie* to find Grandpa Levy out in front, smoking a Winston.

"Cherie," Papa addressed Mommy. "I'll let you and the kids out and go park the car." Mommy nodded. When I climbed out of the backseat, Grandpa walked up and shook my hand. He always shook my hand like a business acquaintance, but I know he adored me. Luc jumped headfirst into his arms, "Grampy!"

"Where's Mom?" Mommy asked Grandpa.

"She's inside talking to the rabbi. Benjamin and Karen are at the bar."

Mommy took Luc's hand and they made their way in. I waited with Grandpa to finish his cigarette which was around the time that Papa came from the parking lot down the street. He looked strikingly handsome in his suit. He was my Papa, and I was madly in love with him. He shook Grandpa's hand.

"Hi, Dad."

"Hiya," Grandpa said, shaking it hard.

La Vie was closed to the public for our private party. It felt strange for all of the tables which were usually so full with patrons to be so empty, still elegantly set.

A man from Argentina named Luis tended bar for the party. Raj, Papa's head chef, was in the kitchen prepping all of the food: frizee lettuce with fresh bacon in a vinaigrette, coq au vin, steak frites, salmon with mustard sauce, rosemary potatoes, crème brûlée for dessert. Luis kept smiling at me. He asked me if I wanted a Shirley Temple. I nodded, smiling back and watched him blend grenadine and ginger ale, and set a maraschino cherry on top. Grandpa drank his regular Scotch and water, Grandma a Virgin Mary, Mommy and Papa, Uncle Benjamin and Karen, red wine, Luc a Coke.

The rabbi had married my parents ten years earlier. He might have wondered what he was doing back there with them, whether the need for this was more than some undying passion my parents held for one another. My guess is that he didn't ask too many questions and that they didn't offer up too many answers.

My mother wore her original wedding dress. What I can't say is whether she held her original optimism.

CHAPTER ELEVEN

FOR A WHILE, I thought of the ski trip to Colorado as a turning point in my family's history. My mother's right foot hurt her for as long as I could remember, but there was never any sort of diagnosis, or a doctor who had a clue what to do for her. She'd visited innumerable doctors through the years of my childhood, searching for a clear answer to the source of the pain, recalling to them a ski accident she was involved in at the age of seventeen. Up in Killington, Vermont, with some girlfriends of hers, she'd twisted her foot the wrong way and she attributed the pain to that event, as it was the only explicable thing.

I was twelve and Luc was eight. We were on our first family trip out West. We drove to the Club Med Resort from Denver in a taxi van with another family that was going skiing for the week. I felt weird since we'd landed, not myself . . . shaky and lightheaded and a little unreal.

"It's the altitude," Mommy said, assuring me that my body would quickly adjust to its new distance from the sky, but my strange feelings lasted. A piercing pain ran through each of my ears. Papa refuted my claim that my ear drums had popped. He insisted that if they had, I would be bleeding. My head was rested in Mommy's lap, and I opened my eyes only sporadically, drifting in and out of consciousness.

"Look!" I heard Luc say distantly. We were still on flat land but inching toward mountains that loomed wondrously, soaring into the Colorado night. The sky was peppered with the brightest stars I'd ever seen. The taxi driver who met us in Denver headed toward a tunnel chiseled through rock that carried us in the dark for what seemed like several minutes. It was Space Mountain at Disneyland, but there were no drops that made my heart fall through my stomach.

I was still convinced that my ear drums had popped when we finally arrived at the resort and checked into our suite, a door connecting the room I shared with Luc to Mommy and Papa's room. After a bath, I sank into the hotel sheets, exhausted from the trip. Mommy and Papa both came to kiss me goodnight, leaving the bathroom light between the two rooms on.

"Kiki," Papa said, "you'll feel much better tomorrow. We're going to have a great day skiing."

There was no transition between consciousness and sleep. When I woke to sunlight streaming into the hotel room the next morning, my ears were still throbbing. I was too sick to ski. Papa said that he would miss me. Mommy put the television on for me so I'd feel like I had some company. When I woke up again hours later, still feverish, Mommy was there to tell me the good news.

"Uncle Benjamin and Aunt Karen had their baby this morning! He's a healthy little boy whose name is Cory." Her eyes started to tear.

"Why are you crying?" I asked her.

"I'm just happy. People don't just cry when they are sad."

"Oh."

"Or maybe I'm a little sad because they live all the way in Los Angeles now, and I won't get to see Cory grow up."

"They'll visit. We'll visit," I consoled her.

"I know—you're right."

Mommy had trouble skiing that she didn't anticipate. We'd been skiing before in Vermont, and the pain in her foot hadn't acted up. This time was different. She and Papa were on a Black Diamond slope when her foot spasmed and she fell. She slid for a while, the boot derailed from the ski.

"What happened?" Papa asked, catching up to her. He removed her boot to see if there was blood. There wasn't.

This was the story that repeated itself like a dream. The characters and the plot remained the same, while the scenery was variable.

"*Ma poule,*" Papa said. "We need to get you back to the lodge."

"I can't move. I can't ski back."

At a loss for what to do, Papa was relieved when mountain patrol arrived, and Mommy was brought back to the main ski lodge on a snowmobile.

There was a man whose existence worked its way into my consciousness for the remainder of our vacation week in Colorado. Something about him provoked my suspicion, although he was probably a very good man. I didn't like seeing him with my mother though, apart from my father.

"He's a surgeon," Mommy explained to me. "I told him about my bad foot, and he may be able to help me out."

Dr. Rabinowitz advised Mommy to stay off her swollen foot for the rest of the week. She and I went to the spa together. We wore our matching polka-dot bikinis, and frequented the Jacuzzi, steam room, and sauna.

"It's a good thing I have you around," Mommy said. "You always cheer me up. You're really very uplifting."

CHAPTER TWELVE

A FEW MONTHS of quiet preceded my parent's trip to Baltimore when Dr. Rabinowitz would surgically open up Mommy's foot to determine the real source of her problem. Rather than find a doctor in New York, where we lived, Mommy and Papa went on this odyssey down south. They had faith in Dr. Rabinowitz, believing that he was the one who finally would find the answer.

Grandma and Grandpa took Luc and me to their Hamptons house on the weekend that they went down to Baltimore.

The Hamptons house was one of the happiest settings of my youth. On some weekends, the whole family came out. Those weekends were my favorite. Papa prepared the food, and Grandpa barbequed it in the gigantic backyard filled with trees and wildflowers. Mommy wore sundresses and helped Grandma set the outdoor picnic table.

The house was quaint and painted a grayish blue on its exterior. There was one level where the real rooms were, and a dingy, moldy basement where Luc and I rode tricycles when we were smaller, creating a bike rink around the dirty pipes that ran from ceiling to floor.

In the large backyard were a sun deck and an orange hammock that hung between two trees where everyone took sun naps. Grandpa always swung me in it. An outdoor shower was attached to the house where you stood on knobby, gray pebbles as you soaped and shampooed yourself in the fresh Long Island air.

Each of the bedrooms of the house had a name, coined by Grandma and determined simply by the paint color on the wall. The "blue room" was hers and Grandpa's, the largest in the house by far. The walls were twilight blue and there were two single beds pushed together, made separately with separate sets of twin sheets and blankets. This was different from the way Mommy and Papa slept. It was an unusual experience crawling into bed with my grandparents after a nightmare or just wanting closeness midway through the night. I couldn't travel in their bed as I could in my parent's bed on one side of them or in between them.

The distinguishing feature of the blue room was the old, black piano that was once in Grandma's apartment growing up as a girl in Bensonhurst, Brooklyn. Grandma's mother was a piano teacher who schooled many of the Jewish girls in the neighborhood. Grandma taught me all she knew from her own mother. We played "*Heart and Soul*" together, side by side at the piano and then I couldn't stop singing it.

The "green room" had lime-green walls, which were

nearly a fluorescent shade, and a single bed with a pullout beneath it. Luc and I slept in there together if the yellow room was taken. In the green room was this picture of a clown. Grandma always said that it was a present from a teacher she worked with at the junior high in Queens she taught at before she retired, but I had my own story about the clown that I believed to be true. In my version, there was a little girl who lived several blocks from the blue house on Tyrone Drive. Her house had many steep steps that climbed up to a bright red front door. Inside the house, the little girl, who was my age, lived with her Grandmother, who was an artist. She was the little girl next to the clown in the picture; her Grandmother had sold us the painting.

"Sweetheart," Grandma said to me, "you dreamed this." She insisted that the little girl didn't exist, but I knew I had met her . . . I was sure of it.

The "yellow room" was where Mommy and Papa slept if they were there. Its window overlooked the outdoor shower. Admittedly, I took sneak peaks of almost everyone nude and never got caught!

The double bed in the yellow room creaked when you sat on it and on the bureau was a music box that played "*Für Elise*" by Beethoven when opened, a song that my piano teacher in Roslyn, Mr. Glick, taught me to play.

The yellow room was also where Luc was conceived. Papa loved to tell the story of the day that Mommy got pregnant with him. Privately it embarrassed me and it defi-nitely mortified Mommy when he told it because her cheeks reddened and she pushed his arm and scolded, "Remy! Stop it!"

They were out in the Hamptons for the weekend alone. Papa wanted to pull the car over and do it in the woods but Mommy was too shy, so they came back to the yellow room and achieved their goal of a new life.

The weekend that Mommy and Papa were in Baltimore, the yellow room was mine. At this critical juncture of becoming a young woman, I wanted a room all to myself. While sleepovers with Luc were once preferable, I'd started to crave my solitude.

"Your sister is growing up," Grandma told Luc. "She's starting to be a real lady. She wants her privacy now. Don't be insulted."

To make Luc feel better, I stayed in the green room with him until he fell asleep. I told stories and jokes with him, looking forward to getting to my own wide, creaky double bed.

Grandma never cared if we stayed up late, while Mommy, who was much more regimented and prone to panic when schedules were abandoned, would never let us stay up as late. "Kids. I can still hear you!" Five minutes later. "Kids. It's time to stop talking and get to bed!"

Grandma and I watched Hitchcock's *Vertigo*. We played badminton on the front lawn and took walks to the bay. I carved sculptures out of wood with Grandpa's tools in the garage. I visited the next-door neighbors Marilyn and Marvin. Marilyn liked to eat Milano cookies and play gin rummy at her kitchen table. Marvin had a massive collection of carved owls in a room called "The Florida Room," each of which he had carved and varnished himself.

Grandma got angry when I called my girlfriends in Roslyn.

"Calls are expensive," she said.

Papa always said that the Great Depression went to both of my grandparents's heads.

"Your grandparents are *obsessed* with money. They are always counting their pennies."

Grandma thought I was taking a nap, but I was calling my friends from the phone, talking stealthily under the covers.

"What are you laughing at?" she tapped at the door during one of my conversations.

"I was just thinking about something funny," I called.

"Don't you think you should get up soon? We're going to go to dinner."

"Okay," I said, waiting until she walked back down the hall to say goodbye to my friend.

It was muggy. The mosquitoes were out, finding me, leaving red, itchy lumps everywhere on my skin.

"They like you because you're pretty," Grandpa said, wandering over to his bathroom medicine cabinet to find a tube of Rhuli cream. It looked and felt like toothpaste, stained my clothes an ugly orange, but stopped the itch.

"Does the job," Grandpa said. "Does the job."

Grandma and Grandpa insisted on the early-bird special at Gosman's Dock Restaurant in Montauk, the town at the easternmost point of Long Island. At five, we loaded into the velvet-seated Buick. I felt the breeze in my hair, savoring the ride as we moved closer to the sea, the sand dunes, the driftwood, and the sticky salty air. The day was perfect.

We were seated at Gosman's, an ocean-front table, no competition, since we were the first ones there. I ordered Shrimp in a Basket—eight plump shrimp with tangy, tartar sauce and fries, grabbing all of Luc's fries, too, because he was the only American child who despised French Fries.

"What an appetite!" Grandpa laughed at me, sipping his customary cup of Manhattan clam chowder.

"Papa says I have the appetite of a horse."

"Growing girls should have big appetites," Grandpa laughed. On the car ride on our way back to the house on Tyrone Drive, we had our usual sing-along, singing Grandpa's seafood song first: "Hold Tight," a song he used to sing with his army buddies.

Mommy and Papa returned from Baltimore several hours after Grandma and Grandpa brought me and Luc back from the Hamptons to Roslyn. Grandma was brewing coffee in the kitchen, slicing Entenmanns's pound cake, when the Mercedes pulled into the garage. She remained in the kitchen with Grandpa while Luc and I rushed out to the car, yanking open the passenger door seat to kiss and hug Mommy.

"Watch out!" Mommy shrieked, shielding her bad foot draped in bandages with her hands.

Papa asked Luc to grab Mommy's new crutches from

the trunk and transport them into the house. He cradled Mommy in his arms and carried her inside as Grandma held open the screen door where she waited.

"Where do you want to sit, Cherie?" he asked her.

"In the living room."

Everyone hovered around him as he carried her inside and mounted her bad foot on one of the designer throw pillows that matched our green, suede couch.

"Did you have a nice time in the Hamptons?" Mommy asked. She was smiling, attempting to display interest and enthusiasm despite the pain, trying not to grimace.

"Yes . . . did they find out what was wrong with you?" I asked.

"There's a problem, but Doctor Rabinowitz isn't sure yet what it is."

"Is anyone hungry?" Papa asked.

When everyone voted unanimously for Chinese food, Luc volunteered to go with Papa to pick up the order.

I'm not sure where either Grandma or Grandpa ventured off to, but somehow I was alone in the living room with my mother.

"Are you going to die?" I asked her.

"Don't be silly," she laughed, her short, nervous laugh. "Why would you ask me something like that?"

I didn't know why I'd have asked her something like that, what would have prompted my question other than a fear, the fear that every child has, that a parent could die. Now and then, I defined to myself what "die" meant. *To die is to no longer exist. When someone dies, you don't ever see them again.*

I said it out loud, unsure of why I defined it for myself when I knew the definition. Perhaps it was because even for a girl of twelve, the concept was hard to grasp.

The adults discretely slipped into the library after we ate Chinese food in the kitchen. Luc vanished into another wing of the house, planting himself in one of his favorite places—inches from the television set in the den. The Disney Sunday movie was on.

I cleaned the dishes in the kitchen and when I finished, I braved the hallway to the library, a room perched at the far left end of our house. The library was the room where the adults convened for private conversations. Those conversations always aroused my curiosity. The opaque curtain on the library's door hid me, as I pressed my ear right up against the glass for clues.

"Rabinowitz said the tumor was the size of a golf ball," Papa said, his voice suddenly lowering. It was as if he knew I was there, felt me spying through that curtain: I was an apparition haunting him, craving to hear more, unable to, then hearing only some incomprehensible mumbling.

I looked tumor up in the World Book Encyclopedia that Grandpa Levy bought me for my tenth birthday; it differentiated between benign and malignant. Benign was safe. Malignant was dangerous. This research was how I realized that Mommy might not be safe any longer, that I might not be able to protect her. I couldn't love her enough to safeguard her. I couldn't pray to God enough to be assured that she'd be out of harm's way.

She came to my bedroom to say goodnight after Grandma and Grandpa went home, struggling to maneuver herself around on her new crutches. I asked her for a story.

"You're too grown up for a story." She laughed. "You'll be thirteen in a couple of weeks!"

"No, Mom. Please. Tell me a story. Tell me a Mitzi."

Tell Me a Mitzi was a book she'd read me countless times when I was younger. It was a tale about a little girl who made a trip completely alone across a city to get to her Grandmother's house just to be told a story.

"Okay," Mommy giggled. " You have the best memory in the world, remembering that book. You must have been five when I read that to you."

"So . . . tell me a Mitzi," I said.

She told me the story that she told me when she was just too worn-out to tell me a more lengthy story.

"Once upon a time there was a madman who had a mad wife and two mad children and that's the end of the story. Good night."

I laughed. She kissed me softly on the cheek. I hugged her tightly to be sure that the imprint would stay, the imprint of her soft arms around me, making me whole.

CHAPTER THIRTEEN

LUC SPIED as much as I did, though Mommy had always warned both of us never to spy.

"If you spy, one day you will hear something that you don't want to hear."

It was not long after Mommy and Papa returned from Baltimore when Luc picked up the ringing phone at the same time as Mommy, hearing Uncle Benjamin's voice on the other end.

"Hang up, Luc," she instructed, but Luc disobeyed her. He tricked her to think he was gone by clicking the mute button on and off. He alerted me to the information he heard when I arrived home from volleyball practice well after seven P.M. that evening, shortly before dinner time.

"Dr. Rabinowitz wants Mommy to have her leg or her foot amputated. She doesn't want to. She said she doesn't want us to have a cripple for a mother, that she won't be an invalid."

"What did Uncle Benjamin say?"

"He said that we'd rather have a mother with a handicap than no mother at all."

"Would you be embarrassed if Mommy was crippled?" I asked Luc.

"No. Would you?" he demanded.

"A little." It wasn't the answer that he wanted to hear, but I was being honest with him.

"I love Mommy no matter what," he snapped.

I was ashamed . . . sickened with myself for letting it pass through my mind for a second that it would be preferable for Mommy to die than for her to be crippled. I believed it was a terrible thought that God would punish me for; God would read my mind and God would make me pay.

Truthfully, though, Mommy had no intentions of becoming handicapped. She informed us in time about Dr. Rabinowitz's suggestion, while never mentioning his ultimatum, which was that she had little chance of surviving without an immediate amputation. Grandma and Grandpa advised her to get "second opinions," which became third, fourth, and fifth opinions. Eventually she found the doctor she hoped for who told her that she could keep her leg.

CHAPTER FOURTEEN

FIRST THERE WERE outpatient visits for radiation rays. The doctors put X marks on her foot with a permanent marker, branding her a patient. A bulge developed where the rays were directed, which turned purple and grotesque. She asked me nearly every day when I arrived home from school if I thought that the tumor looked smaller from the treatments. I nodded. While I said yes to please her, I knew privately that the tumor was growing bigger.

She began chemo treatment several months later. Sometimes she was trapped in a hospital bed for over a week. Papa hired housekeepers from the Caribbean islands to maintain the house and to keep an eye on me and Luc after school. They cooked for us if he couldn't make it home in time from work to make us something. I learned then to enjoy the taste of jerk chicken and yellow rice while missing the comfort of my mother's food.

When Papa got home from work in the evenings, we went to visit her. We never skipped a night. We brought her the bland Chinese food that she requested that wouldn't make her feel nauseated. She devoured the egg-drop soup and white rice readily, always thrilled that we brought it.

I call to mind the heartrending pull of leaving her there alone when we had to go back home, nudged by Papa that we had school tomorrow. I remember walking down the shiny, linoleum hallways of the hospital wing, sullen, back to the parking lot, imagining that she might be crying, scared, left to the company of the television set, which hung midway through the air above her bed. She was left to the comfort of nurses. They were strangers who showed her the utmost empathy and care, but were not her family. I knew she just wanted to be home, taking care of us.

I call to mind those silent rides when I sat in the passenger seat next to Papa, in her place. I felt a scary twinge of the unknown and a perpetual nostalgia. I wished back for the yesterdays that I hadn't appreciated when there was health in my home.

I call to mind being ashamed to cry in front of Papa and Luc, waiting to cry until I found the safety of my sheets and the raggedy dolls that filled my twin, girlhood bed.

For many months, there was just no talk at all of what this was called. I knew its name, but it felt somehow that if I didn't say the word, it couldn't exist, exert its negative power. The World Book Encyclopedia had spelled it out clearly enough on the night Mommy and Papa came home from Baltimore; a malignancy was cancer. But months seemed to go by before Papa confessed to me and Luc that which I had already suspected.

"Mommy has cancer," he whispered, standing next to the Thomas McKnight painting in our dining room with the green glass chandelier, the black marble table, and the shiny white wood floors. He spoke to us as if in treachery, betraying Mommy's wish to keep the name of her disease secret, so that we wouldn't feel afraid.

During Papa's confession, Mommy was in her bedroom resting. She spent much of the day doing that, never feeling healthy even when the chemo was over. She dreaded heading back to the hospital for treatments, but every four weeks, like clock work, she packed up her 1970s, circular red valise, and a trooper, she went. I admired her for her bravery and didn't tell her so enough times. I saw firsthand that chemotherapy was a torturous thing to endure. I watched her suffer selflessly for me, Luc, and Papa. She was determined never to let cancer get the best of her. There was an astounding dignity about how she handled herself. She rarely ever complained about what she had to undergo. I admired her resilience, sure that if it were I, I would not have fought for my own life with such tenacity.

CHAPTER FIFTEEN

IT WAS MY EIGHTH-GRADE GRADUATION; I'd be fourteen in July. Mommy had no hair and wore terrycloth caps around her head at home. When she went out, she either wore satin scarves that Grandma bought her or the totally hideous wig from the wig shop in Forest Hills, Queens. I hated that wig. I thought it looked fake and made her head look oddly shaped. It lacked the flow and healthy shine of her once fine, dark, brunette hair.

Mommy didn't let anyone see her bald, including Papa. I only saw her bald head once, and it was entirely by accident. I'd gone into my parents' room to sleep on the cot near their bed after having a nightmare. When I looked at Mommy in bed, I saw that the yellow, terrycloth cap that she went to sleep with had fallen halfway across her head. Her scalp was left only with dark wisps of hair. Her head looked like a bald doll that some wicked child tried to yank all the hair out of, unable to yank every last strand.

I was more popular at school than I had been in grade school, fully in control of my own style. Papa no longer policed my wardrobe and gave me full reign over my outfit choices. Looking more the part at school helped me gain acceptance.

Lots of kids at Roslyn Middle School knew that Mommy had cancer. Mommy speculated now and then out loud to me and Luc about exactly how the word got out. She wondered who of the few friends that she told had leaked her confidential information. She was skeptical of the people she was closest to, paranoid that they may have deceived her. We never did figure out how so many people knew, but somehow they did.

Being the sick mother's daughter in town awarded me sympathy and even some new alliances. Sometimes I liked it. I felt privileged, special by default. But mostly it unnerved me to receive empathetic glances, pitying eyes on me. I could read people's minds; I knew what they were thinking. *I'm glad it's not my family.* For reasons that I can only speculate about, I felt most awkward around my friends's mothers. The way they looked at me made me feel ashamed. Perhaps it was because I felt like they could see into me with sharper clarity, more piercing strength than fathers could, or even my peers. They knew most clearly just what I was missing because *they* were what I was missing. They were healthy women, able to run around at their kid's beck and call. An already existing inadequacy I felt because Papa always wanted me to be different, had sharpened. It had formed into a more acute sense of alienation.

I knew Mommy would have preferred not to come to the graduation on her crutches, in her wig. I knew that she had to push herself. I wanted her there, but I was anxious about people seeing her. I kept these feelings to myself but Papa knew about them. He was a mind reader, always reading my mind. He was furious at me for feeling the shame

I felt. He thought I was despicable, and so I felt that I must indeed be despicable.

My heart started beating frantically as the Mercedes drove slowly over the safety speed bumps of the school parking lot where the graduation was held. All of the parents and their children were loading out of cars, approaching the entrance of the school. The healthy mothers and fathers were dressed royally. They wore Rolex watches, Benetton outfits. Name brands. Everywhere in sight were parked Porsches, Mercedeses, and BMWs. The parking lot was a flaunting of nouveau riche Long Island wealth. Graduation . . . Translation: Fashion Show: Competition. Who had more money to showcase? Papa was a player in the game though he pretended that he wasn't. He cared about sporting pricey possessions just as many of the other parents did, but he still snickered about the Roslyn snobs and showoffs.

"Here they are. The stupid Roslyn japs."

"Okay Remy," Mommy said. "Enough. Don't ruin the night."

Mommy never cared much for fashion and when she was sick, she cared even less than before. Her shirt didn't really match her pants, and I worried what people would be thinking.

Not only is her mother sick but she can't match for her life—she has no sense of style.

As soon as Papa parked the car, I ran off. I found a

friend of mine named Sandi and her family. I wanted to melt into them and be part of their visibly healthy family. Out of the corner of my eye, I saw Mommy and Papa head into the school's auditorium with Luc, finding seating in the back rows. Mommy wanted as little attention drawn to her as possible. She was friendly when people approached her, but I saw through her act whenever I glanced over at her. She wanted to sit where she could make a quick getaway. She wouldn't really leave, but she wanted to position herself in a place where she could.

Terry and Jamie from the Great Neck apartment building who had since moved to Roslyn approached me as I stood with Sandi's family. They had already seen Mommy and Papa and Luc.

"Your mom looks great," Jamie said. I didn't know if she was telling me the truth. But I thought that Mommy looked horrible, compared to how she once looked. She just was not pretty as she once was, her face pale and eyes sunken.

I eyed my parents from my alphabetically correct seat on the stage once all were seated for the ceremony. I sat in the front row on a blue fold-up chair, hot in my overheated cap and gown; the band began "The Star-Spangled Banner." Mommy smiled and waved at me. Papa scowled at me, delivering a telepathic message.

How dare you run away from us? We are your family. Sandi and her parents are not. How dare you run away from us, you little bitch? How dare you be ashamed?

I *was* filled with shame about my family, but far worse

was the shame I felt toward myself. Were I a better child, I'd not have been ashamed. Were I a more worthy and empathetic human being, I'd not have felt the way I did. Were I truly special, I'd have relinquished all care of how anyone judged us.

I walked to them hesitantly after the ceremony's end, when all two hundred students in my grade were handed paper diplomas and encouraged happily on to high school, all sorts of slogans about how the world was your oyster. Mommy and Papa remained in their rows, wanting to remain carefully removed from commotion. Luc had run off with some friends who had older brothers and sisters in my grade.

"Congratulations," Mommy beamed. I kissed her, then Papa on the cheek. He moved his face away.

"Should we go for ice cream?" Mommy said. "Remy?" She tugged his arm.

"No. Let's go home."

"Ice cream would be nice," she pressed.

"We don't need ice cream."

It was not to punish her, but me, for running to Sandi's family from the car, for wanting another family to claim as my own.

"If you want ice cream . . ." Papa snarled, "go find Sandi's parents and ask them to take you and Sandi."

"Stop it Remy," Mommy begged. "It's a good night. A good night."

We drove back to the house in silence. I felt that I caused it all. I set off my father. Something defective in me provoked his rage. I was able to induce such hatred in him. I had the power to elicit evil and that further crushed my self worth.

I headed straight to my bedroom when we arrived home and remained there through bedtime. Mommy came in a while after, and sat down on my bed next to me.

"I'm really sorry that we didn't go for ice cream."

"It's okay."

"I'll make it up to you."

"You don't have to. It wasn't your fault. I just was excited to see Sandi. I don't know why he's so mad."

"You know how he gets," she said. I nodded. We both knew how he got. We shared that special knowledge. But he was more and more of a loose cannon these days, always aimed at me.

"I love you," Mommy said.

"Papa doesn't."

"Of course he does. He loves you. Don't be silly." She kissed me, reached for her crutches and exited slowly. Tears were bubbling that waited to spill from my eyes when she was gone from the room.

This void had appeared inside me. It was a throbbing, vacuumlike hole carved into my chest, below my throat, spreading through the pit of my stomach. It never left me. I was missing her as if she were already gone.

Papa ignored me for weeks. He gave me only basic orders. His withholding of love furthered my shame. It nurtured a space within me that housed the belief that I was bad. I'd been ashamed of a helpless mother who could barely walk, drive, or live as she used to. A mother who waited for the day her hair would grow back, claiming when it did she'd grow it long, like Rapunzel. I despised myself, and contemplated my own evil; only an evil child could have been embarrassed by her sick mother. Only a deranged child, not one with a heart, could ever feel as I did.

Each evening when I heard the garage door open, alerting me to his arrival home, I prayed that something in him had clicked, that he'd feel some sense of mercy for me. But his eyes were glazed over when he spoke to me, as if I were a stranger.

I went down to the den one evening after dinner to find him playing his guitar. The song he played this time was *"Angie."* The Rolling Stones. He looked at me oddly as if I were a mutant creature that he felt totally alienated by. I was not his creation; I was this child who through some mandated obligation of the law he had to feed and clothe, but he was doing so against his will.

"Yes?" he requested from me in a matter of fact way, like a bank clerk pressed for time.

"Why are you so angry at me?"

He paused before he spoke.

"It angers me that you are ashamed of your mother."

"I'm not," I said.

"Yes. You are. I know you. I know everything you think and feel. I *made* you. Remember?"

"Well, I'm not ashamed of her," I choked.

"Go tell that to your mother."

"She's not the one mad at me. *You are.*"

"She may not be angry," he said, "but deep down inside, she's hurting because of you. Because you're selfish."

His words stained my insides with a stubborn and irremovable psychic tar that could be scraped and scraped at but never removed fully. I walked out of the den. Mommy was upstairs on her bed. She was stitching an Afghan blanket. I lay down next to her and held her hand.

"I love you Mommy. Do you know that?"

"Of course I do. Don't be silly. Of course I know that you love me," she assured me and smiled. I wondered whether she was just saying it . . . whether she believed it. I feared that I had worsened her pain.

CHAPTER SIXTEEN

THE NARRATIVES OF HOPE ended abruptly. An imaginary line in my mind delineates the before and the after. In the before, my mother could get better . . . in the after, she could not. There were three years of the before, and three days of the after.

It was March of 1991, just a few months before my fifteenth birthday. Mommy had been very irritable lately. She had a fit because I ripped an Absolut ad out of a magazine that was sitting on the rack alongside side of her bed. (It was trendy at my school at the time to collect Absolut ads.) I thought I was being nice by spending time with her, but everything I did pissed her off.

"That's my magazine," she snapped.

"That's my magazine," I mimicked.

"Don't mimic me."

"Don't mimic me."

"Get out of here, will you!"

"Bitch," I yelled, slamming her bedroom door as I exited. Aunt Karen heard the commotion down in the kitchen. She was making Mommy a sandwich. Surprisingly, she and Uncle Benjamin and Cory had flown in from L.A. to stay with us for a while. They slept in our guest room with the cedar closet that smelled like mothballs and the two twin beds with floral bedspreads.

I headed across the hall to my room, banging my own door shut so fiercely that the mirror screwed to the door unlatched. It fell but didn't break. I lay face down on my pillow, my hands over my head, kicking my feet against the bed in frustration.

Aunt Karen knocked but I ignored her. She came in anyway and sat down next to me, taking my hand.

"What happened?" she asked.

"Mommy is being impossible. She's cranky every time I go to spend time with her. She cares more about her magazines and whether I rip pages out than how my day was at school. Why should I spend time with her if she's going to be such a bitch?"

"You know," Aunt Karen began, about to impart words

of wisdom to me that I never forgot. "Your mother's life is confined to a very small space: her bed. When your life is confined to such a small space the things in that space seem to matter more. Do you understand what I mean?"

I nodded. What she said made sense. She squeezed my hand and looked me straight in the eyes, a truth-teller finally, still allowing a small window of hope with her words. "Your mother might die," she said. "Do you know that?"

I think some place inside me I did know . . . of course it had entered my mind that it could happen, but for so long everyone said that with the treatments she could heal and that she could keep fighting the cancer. Until Aunt Karen said what she said, the bad time Mommy was having was only a downswing. We had downswings before. It didn't mean she was dying. It just meant that she was very sick.

But Aunt Karen was trying to warn me because no one else was planning to. She was trying to give me fair notice so that I would be able to process the pain without as much shock. But then it all happened so quickly. Like two cars colliding. You can't think before the crash.

Mommy's health rapidly declined; she had nightly panic attacks where she woke up screaming. A member of Hospice Care came to sleep at our house. I heard her yelling at Grandma and Grandpa, Papa, Uncle Benjamin, Karen in her bedroom. I spied on the conversation with my ear up against a drinking glass that I pressed against the door.

"Hospice Care is for the terminally ill," Mommy raged. "You are all giving up on me. That's very nice."

We didn't talk, have a heart to heart. She didn't tell me that she would be leaving me, mostly because she did not believe that she would be. She would not surrender willingly. Death would capture her against her will.

Papa decided that Luc and I should not stay at home. I didn't say goodbye to Mommy. I just packed my backpack, and Grandma ushered me out to the car where Mommy's friend Ronda and her husband Joel were waiting.

Ronda and Joel didn't tell me that she would fine, that she'd get through this hump. No one was telling lies anymore. They took us home in their Volkswagen. Their children welcomed us, made us laugh, made our fear more bearable. Luc and I slept next to each other, under blankets in the living room. The living room had a fireplace and a skylight which looked out to a beautiful garden where Ronda always built the Sukkoth house. The Wolfs's house was a place I'd once felt safe, but I felt safe nowhere now. I felt alone. No soft blankets, no reassuring words brought me any true peace. I didn't know if I would ever see Mommy again. I didn't think I would. Next time I went home, she would not be there. Ronda tapped me softly at 4 A.M., our second night of staying there.

"Your Papa wants us to bring you home now. To say goodbye to your mom. She's not going to make it through the night."

I brushed my teeth, not changing into day clothes.

"Just put your coat on over your pajamas," Ronda said.

Neither Luc nor I were crying. Ronda and Joel didn't

speak as we drove. There was nothing to say, really, so I just breathed against the moist window.

Luc and I visited Mommy separately. I went in first with one of the Hospice nurses, a Jamaican woman named Ruthie. There was a brown oxygen machine the size of an air conditioner next to Mommy's bed, linked up to plastic tubes that fed air into her nose. Her lips had a bluish tint, and the skin on them was ripped.

"I don't know what to say," I told Ruthie.

"Tell her that you love her and that she'll always be in your heart."

"I love you Mommy, and you'll always be in my heart," I repeated robotically. Her eyes flashed open, just momentarily.

"She heard you," Ruthie exclaimed. "She definitely heard you." I kissed her soft cheek goodbye.

We were only back at Ronda and Joel's for a while when Mommy died. Luc had fallen asleep briefly and then sat up screaming for her. He was trapped in some sort of temporary delirium. Ronda and Joel couldn't get him out of the state; he was too far in. When he finally stopped screaming, like clockwork, the phone rang. It was Papa, telling Ronda and Joel that she was dead. They didn't tell us, but I knew what the ringing phone meant and I lay awake, stiff. The long, unpleasant era of numbness toward Mommy began. The next morning when Papa arrived at the door, my body had no sensation. I was not crying. He walked Luc and me out to the garden and sat down with us, holding each of ours hands.

"Mommy is pain free now," he said. "Uncle Benjamin

and I took her to the morgue last night in some blankets from the cedar closet."

I didn't understand why I was frozen. I thought it was probably because I was a bad child, a cold and insensitive bitch, just like Papa had said I was. I didn't really love Mommy. I was ashamed of her when she was entirely help-less. Now my punishment from God was that I couldn't feel a thing at all.

A girl in the sky watched me. Soon she watched Mommy's body lowered into the ground. She watched me stand di-vided from my family. She observed me, a lone entity who would now fend for herself. The girl in the sky told me very matter-of-factly that there was no real safety left in the world, that all the safety in the world was gone.

Part Two
Papa

CHAPTER SEVENTEEN

Mother's Day fell around six weeks after she died. When I woke up that morning it was overcast. Gray light seeped into my bedroom. I remember lingering in bed for a while before I reached for the phone to call Grandma. This holiday would never be fun for either of us again. She'd always be the mother without a daughter, and I'd be the daughter without a mother. Daughters and mothers were irreplaceable things, she'd pointed out to me, also sharing her belief that losing a daughter was much worse than losing a mother because it defied the natural course of things. In my view, Mommy's untimely death also defied the natural course of things, but I didn't argue with her point.

Grandma answered the phone, her voice glum. Mother's Day alone would have been enough to explain her bleak mood, but I found out soon enough that Papa had done something to upset her and Grandpa: something insensitive and ruthless. While it was not uncharacteristic of him to do something that would hurt somebody's feelings, I couldn't help being shocked by what Grandma told me.

He'd called her that morning to tell her that she and Grandpa were no longer invited to come over to the house for the day because he was having a "Mother's Day" party to which they were not invited.

"A party?" I asked her incredulously.

"Yes," she said. "He said that we'd be out of place."

So he was hosting a Mother's Day party without the mother . . . my mother. I wondered whether he'd gone temporarily insane. This was certainly the most outlandish thing he'd ever managed to cook up, and while it didn't really go against the grain of what he'd proclaimed to me and Luc was his new motto, I still found it unfathomable.

"Life is about me now," he'd told us. "Remember that." His eyes were bloodshot and cruel.

"Papa! Papa! Where are you?" I yelled into the tranquil house when I hung up with Grandma, hearing only the echo of my own voice "Papa!"

I searched for him everywhere, noticing that the door of the library that led outside had been left wide open. The library led into the greenhouse, which led to a stone path. The path was carved through an area of shrubbery and flowers that ended at our swimming pool. Lilies of the valley were out. I smelled their delicate scent, flooding me with the memory of Papa picking them from the garden for Mommy to tie into her barrettes. Bees the size of grapes flew through the air. Their buzzing made me cringe. I brushed them away from my face as I ventured toward the pool, soon hit with the scent of bleach, sun, and wet leaves.

Papa was wearing a pair of briefs, rinsing the lounge chairs down with the garden hose.

"Hi," he said to me, his eyes cold. "I'm glad you're up. I was going to wake you and Luc in a few minutes. I'm taking you guys to the cemetery this morning, and I want to leave here pretty soon."

"I just spoke to Grandma," I said. "Why did you tell her that she and Grandpa can't come over today?"

"I'm having a Mother's Day party here later this afternoon," he confirmed. "Your grandparents aren't invited because they won't fit in with this crowd."

"Who is *this crowd?*"

"Some new friends of mine from the restaurant. No one you know."

"They *need* us today," I said. "Please let them come. Or let them pick up me and Luc and take us out."

"No," he said. The verdict was final. "Don't worry about them. Worry about us instead. Go get your brother up and be ready to leave here in no more than half an hour."

I was familiar with this mood of his. Remote and nasty. It was so vastly different from the sweet side of him, the person who could be generous, empathetic, and warm. I feared him when he was like this. I was his adversary just by existing. He would snap at me if he felt wronged or criticized. He'd glared at me as if I'd asked an inappropriate question, wanting to know why on God's green earth he'd have a Mother's Day party when his children's mother had just died! I had no idea what was going through his mind and that is exactly what made his behavior so baffling to me. If I could have understood it, perhaps it would have been easier to reconcile. It was its mysteriousness that made it the most exasperating.

I walked back into the house to wake up Luc. His bedroom was next door to mine. It was shadier because more of the backyard trees protected his window from the incoming light. He was fast asleep and grinding his teeth when I walked inside. This was not unusual for him—he always ground and he sleepwalked as well. Several days after Mommy died, Papa and I had heard him yelling. We ran into his room to find him in his closet with his blanket and pillows, thinking that he was on a sinking ship, drowning.

I sat down on the red-and-white checkered bedspread and watched him patiently for a while until he opened his large, brown eyes, sensing my presence.

"Hi," he said, yawning.

Finding me in there was not strange. I often came to wake him up or even to sleep next to him if I felt lonely or scared.

"We have to get ready," I said. "We're going to the cemetery in half an hour to visit Mommy."

I walked to his closet and flicked its wall light on, finding a matching shirt and pair of pants for him.

"Papa's crazy," I said. "Completely off the wall."

"Why? What now?" Luc asked. He didn't really want to hear this; it confused him about who Papa was and he needed to trust Papa, more than ever, in Mommy's absence.

"He is having a "Mother's Day" party here today if you can believe it. He told Grandma and Grandpa that they weren't invited over."

"Really?"

"Yeah. Grandma was on the verge of tears when I spoke to her. He was mean to her."

"He must have a reason," Luc said.

"What? What could be a good reason?"

Luc was only ten, but I expected much more from him. I expected the refined wisdom of an adult. I looked to him for insight because I wanted him to be my ally against this new Papa.

"I don't know. I'll talk to him though."

Luc tended to defend Papa while I was always questioning him, armed with a sense of righteousness. I found it maddening that Luc didn't doubt his motives in the way that I did. I could not see the world from his perspective. With the loss of his mother, he needed to believe in his father. Losing trust in Papa would be another loss.

After showering, I put on the same black dress that I wore to Mommy's funeral in April. There was no need for stockings this time—just flat open-toed shoes for the humid May day. I put on lipstick, thinking that I looked pretty for a second in the mirror. I did a double take when I noticed the look in the eyes that stared back at me. They were poignant eyes. Troubled. I was intrigued by them as I stared into them as if there were another girl behind the glass, one I'd never met before . . . a new girl at school whom I wanted to be friends with but was intimidated by.

I met Luc in the kitchen for Honey Nut Cheerios and bananas. He was watching cartoons and even though I thought they were dumb, I couldn't help watching them just because they were there. "G.I. Joe, American Hero," Luc sang.

Papa walked in as we ate. He was drenched from swimming and a beach towel was wrapped around his waist. His olive skin was shiny from his suntan oil, and the kitchen filled quickly with the scent of coconuts.

"Are you two almost ready to go?" he asked, kissing Luc on top of his head. Luc nodded. I scowled.

The silent treatment was my plan. I would let Papa know just how crazy I thought he was by ignoring every last word he said. I would hurt him simply by pretending that he didn't exist.

Luc called shotgun and snagged the passenger seat of the Mercedes. I didn't want it anyhow because I didn't want to sit near Papa. In fact, I wanted to be as far from him as possible. I remember slamming the back door shut and sitting at the far edge of the right corner backseat. I looked angrily through the open window, the wind on my face.

We were on the highway on the way to Mount Lebanon cemetery when Luc broke the silence.

"Why can't Grandma and Grandpa come over today?" he said.

"They won't fit in," Papa told him in a completely reasonable voice. I couldn't continue with the silent treatment any longer. I couldn't let him get away with what he said.

Although I knew what I'd be in for if I questioned his behavior, I was not about to sit there and shut up. Even though I knew that he thought that I was oversensitive. *A real woman. Just like her mother. A bitch if there ever was one.*

"Well, I don't think that I'll *fit in* either," I hissed at him from the backseat.

"Watch it," Papa said. "I'm not in the mood for your attitude today."

"I don't really care."

"Watch it," he repeated. He shook his pointer finger into the rear-view mirror, finding my spiteful glare in the lean, rectangular glass.

"Keep it up and I'll drop you off on the side of the highway."

I knew that he would do it too, without compunction, so I shut my mouth. I didn't want to walk home. I wanted to visit Mommy's grave even though when we arrived, the uncomfortable numbness crept up on me again and the girl in the sky returned.

"Should we get flowers?" Papa asked Luc as he drove off the Expressway, turning onto Myrtle Boulevard, headed toward Mount Lebanon.

"Grandma told me that Jewish cemeteries don't allow flowers," Luc said. "Jews are supposed to put stones."

"Well, that's a stupid rule. Don't you think? I like flowers. Don't you think it would be nice for Mommy to have flowers?"

"I guess," Luc conceded. Papa pulled the Mercedes up

to a bodega and handed him a ten-dollar bill, instructing him to find a pretty bouquet for Mommy.

In my head, there was a countdown—I knew I was up for the kill. Due for another one of his diatribes about how selfish I was.

"You know," he said, "you should really be more of a role model to your brother. He just sees you angry and bitter all the time. He's suffering a lot now. He's only ten and you're not setting much of an example for him with the way that you treat me."

I was humming Guns N' Roses's *"November Rain"* in my head, trying not to listen to his words, trying to keep them from permeating me. I was pretty sure that he was insane, but sometimes I couldn't help wondering if he was right about me. I wondered if even in his craziness he could see the true me: my true colors. Could it be that when people are crazy, they still see some of the truth?

The gatekeeper at the cemetery waved and smiled at Papa, opening the gates. We had memorized the numerous, curvy turns on the narrow roads to get to Mommy's grave. Her stone was on a hill and we had to park on an upward incline. She was buried in my grandmother's family plot. Grandma and Grandpa planned to be buried there one day too.

Her tombstone had the word MOTHER carved across its top surface. On its front it said, "Beloved mother, daughter, and wife. 1948–1991."

I was not me. I was just some girl with someone else's father and brother.

"Go get a stone!" the girl in the sky ordered me, so I wandered to a wooded area near the gravesite and found a large stone. Several smaller stones were placed on the grave, I noticed, when I returned to the grave. This meant that people had been visiting her. I sat on a bench to the right of the grave, staring at the stone. I waited to feel. I waited to cry but my eyes stayed dry. The girl in the sky spoke to me. She asked me why I felt so estranged from myself and why I felt my family was not my family. She told me that normal girls whose mothers that had been dead for six weeks were able to cry. She begged me to cry at least a little, but I couldn't shed a tear.

Papa and Luc sat on a bench of their own, across the way from me.

"Come here," Papa called me, but I ignored him. He was up for the silent treatment again.

"Come sit with us, doll," he urged.

"Your sister is really such a hard head," he said to Luc. He did not say it angrily. It was more like he was making this astute observation about why life was more difficult for me. He believed that I had created all of the struggles that I felt, and I was responsible for the suffering I was feeling. Part of me feared that he was right. The voice of reason told me that he was a stark raving madman.

I finally cried. But I was sure that I was crying because

of him, not because my mother died which worsened my guilt.

"Doll. Come sit with us," he called again, seeing my tears. I sat still, wishing that he and Luc would disappear. I wanted to be alone in the cemetery to talk to my mother. I closed my eyes to shut them out until I heard Papa say that it was time to go home.

The cramps I'd woken up with that morning had worsened. Papa heard me shifting in the backseat, kicking my feet around in frustration.

"What's going on back there?" he asked. "Are you sick?"

"No."

"Do you have your period?" he asked. My cheeks flushed.

"Yes."

"Well, just relax. We'll be home soon."

I stretched out on the leather of the backseat of the car and closed my eyes, sinking into my own weight, my eyes dipped in a warm sea. From the exhaustion of my anger and my cramps, I fell asleep. I woke up to the familiar hum of our garage door lifting.

"Come help me set up for the party Luc," Papa said. Mother's Day. The Mother's Day party without the mother was not just some crazy nightmare. It was still going to happen. Papa was not canceling it. All of the pain I felt had not caused him to call it off. My hurt had not swayed him. I was unimportant.

When I woke up a few hours later, the house was as

quiet as it was that morning. I looked outside from the kitchen window to see a line of unfamiliar cars in our driveway, heading all the way up the small hill in front of our house. As I neared the pool area, I could barely believe what I saw. Topless women were everywhere. Some wore G-strings and carried cocktails or beer bottles. Papa was prancing around jovially in his skin-tight green Speedo. One woman lay completely nude on one of our lounge chairs while a strange man that I'd never seen in my life rubbed suntan lotion onto her ass. A dj booth was set up and music was blasting out into the speakers lined up on the concrete molding. Luc was dancing in the middle of a circle of rowdy dancers. I walked closer, lured by some strange compulsion. Papa spotted me and smiled right at me gloriously as if nothing in the world was wrong with this picture.

"Doll!" he shouted excitedly, ushering me over. "Come here!"

I walked over to him as if I were under a spell, intrigued by what he would say or do. I forgot for a minute how furious I was that all this was taking place. There was something thrilling to me about the party despite my discomfort that it was going on. It's novelty, I suppose.

"Everyone!" he yelled out in French when I reached him. *"C'est ma fille!! Ma belle fille."* ("This is my girl. This is my beautiful girl.") The guests smiled and clapped for me like I had done something to be honored. I was the daughter of the life of the party. Bestowed with applause for being the daughter of this wild, electrifying, party animal.

Papa smelled like beer, sweat, and chlorine. A bar table that was stocked with booze was set up by the pool house. He grabbed me and picked me up as everyone continued clapping, kissing me on the cheek, shaking me with affection. He was in love with me as if our morning trip to Mount Lebanon had never happened.

"Get off me," I said, skirmishing away from him. "Get off." He wouldn't let go.

"I love you. My girl."

"Put me down Papa," I said. "You're drunk." He seized me harder, carrying me to the edge of the poolside and swinging me, teasing to toss me in fully dressed.

"Don't you dare throw me."

"I won't," he laughed, letting me down. "Loosen up, though, doll. Stop being so angry already, will you? Just enjoy the party. Life is very short. Have some food," he said, pointing to the buffet. I walked to the table set off to the side and put some barbequed chicken onto my plate with salad. I poured myself a full glass of white wine as Papa watched me, not saying a word in disapproval.

I called Grandma and Grandpa once back in the house.

"Papa is having a party here at the house with nude women traipsing around the property. And Mommy is flipping in her grave."

"Arthur, pick up," Grandma instructed Grandpa.

"What do you think about that?" I asked Grandpa when he got on the phone.

"I don't know what's wrong with him, but you can't do

anything about it. He's your father. He's the boss. We can't interfere; he's liable to stop us from seeing you if we get involved with his life. He told us not to step on his toes anymore now that your mother is gone."

"He could never stop us from seeing you."

"You'd be surprised. Grandma and I need to stay on his good side. We can't make comments about what he is doing when we're not around."

The drunker I got, refilling my wine glass outside several times, the less I cared about the Mother's Day party. It was only when I woke up queasy the next morning that the sick feeling returned and the questioning of what motivated his actions. This was the piece I could never find, the knowledge I was always searching for.

CHAPTER EIGHTEEN

FREEDOM WAS LIKE AIR: everywhere. There was all the freedom to breathe that I'd ever dreamed of, but it didn't flow easily into my lungs. There was the burning tinge of frosty air. Papa kept going on vacation. He left me and Luc alone in the house for days, sometimes weeks. I suddenly had the type of the freedom that most of my friends were dying for, but the trade-off was that I felt like I didn't matter much. I pretended that it was cool to have no supervision at home, but beneath my pretense I wanted him to care more, to be his priority, to put me and Luc before himself.

We didn't know where he went. He never gave us phone numbers or addresses.

"I'll call you guys," he said, and sometimes he did. He could have been in the town next door or some infinitesimal country at the far end of the world. We knew when he left, but never exactly when he was coming back. He never failed to leave an envelope in the kitchen drawer that said, "Kids: cash." It was crammed with twenty dollar bills, hundreds of dollars worth.

CHAPTER NINETEEN

WEEKDAY AFTERNOONS repeated themselves. The school bus dropped me off at the bottom of my hill, and I walked its steepness lackadaisically, feeling the full weight of the day in my legs, my breath short from the sharp upward climb. When Luc and I were younger we rode our bikes all the way up the hill without taking a single break to breathe. The energy I once had was gone: I'd become a lazy teenager.

I came home to a silent house. Each day when I walked through the front door, I couldn't stop the remembrance of my mother's voice calling me, and my own voice replying.

Is that you?

Yes. Hi, Mom.

I couldn't stop the recollection of finding her somewhere in the house watching soap operas, doing needlepoint or crossword puzzles or sitting in the library drawing on the easel that Papa bought her, listening to the *Les Miserables* soundtrack. A song she listened to quite often toward the end of her life was "I Dreamed a Dream."

In her absence, in that raw aftermath of her death, I kept walking around the house aimlessly. I often found my-self in her room, her closet, or the places in the house that she loved the most. It was as if I was convinced that despite what logic told me, I would find her somewhere if I searched hard enough . . . perhaps there was some remote corner that I still hadn't checked . . . death was merely temporary and eventually I'd make the crucial discovery of where she was.

I wondered where her spirit went and whether or not spirits were real. Papa claimed that he felt something leave the room when she died. He was the one holding her when she breathed her last breath, and he described what left as something gently floating away.

My mind was often on the matter of where we went when we died. It was also on the matter of whether Mommy was okay, if she was conscious somewhere in the afterlife. In the thereafter, was she afraid? Could she be happy if she were away from us? Was she trying to tell me anything, and should I be looking for signs?

Papa called in once in a while when he was on a trip to make sure that Luc and I were okay. He liked to find out that there had been no emergencies.

"Good," he said when I assured him that we were per-fectly fine. "Good." It was as if we served him well by not be-ing involved in any disasters, protecting his liability. I told

Luc that he could get in serious trouble if the authorities knew that he was leaving minor children in a house with no point of contact, completely unsupervised.

"They could chase after him," I insisted, "they could put him in jail." I didn't know if what I was saying was really factual, but I was trying to get him to see eye to eye with me about the neglect I felt was happening to us in my mother's absence. Papa wasn't particularly worried about our staying alone, and he wouldn't let Grandma and Grandpa stay with us when he left. In fact, we were prohibited from telling them that he was even gone at all.

"I don't want them here at the house—patrolling things," he'd said.

To be truthful, I really didn't want them to stay with us either. While Papa had become nonchalant about our safety, Grandma and Grandpa were prone to needless worrying and their neuroses would have been a far worse fate to contend with than Papa's neglect. Life would change from total freedom to total jail. Autonomy . . . complete self determination in the house was the preferable option.

Luc made me angry when he took the spending money from the envelope in the kitchen drawer to buy video games or other types of toys. I tried to blackmail him once by saying that I'd tell Papa how he was taking advantage of our only survival money, but he didn't care. He just stuck out his tongue at me with devilish humor in his eyes and said, "And I'll just tell him you are driving Mommy's car around without a license every night!"

The deal I had with myself was that when I finished all of my homework, I could give myself a reward for working so diligently, for keeping my straight-A average at school. Papa was foolish to leave the keys to Mommy's old gray Peugeot right there on the copper key rack in our kitchen, behind the swinging door. Didn't he know that her car was lonely now that she was gone, and that it needed a driver to keep the seat warm in her place?

It delighted me to get past a cop. It was the time between first spotting the police car as I drove and getting away free that gave me an incredible rush. I thought there might be a guardian angel in that Peugeot with me, cruising around Roslyn. I sensed her presence sometimes. I tested her when I steered onto highways, accelerating fast, holding the wheel with my left hand, fumbling with the radio dial with my right, shutting my eyes for five seconds or more. When I opened them, I was still in my lane, convinced that she must be there. She was looking out for me while I tested the stupid world, saw how far I could get without consequences.

CHAPTER TWENTY

Papa started dating. The cat jumped out of the bag when Luc found a pair of earrings next to the fireplace in our living room and didn't identify them as Mommy's. I didn't recognize them either.

"Whose earrings are these?" he asked Papa as soon as Papa got home from work that evening. I heard them arguing through the frail wall that divided our bedrooms upstairs.

"They belong to a woman named Tracey," he said. "She lives in Los Angeles."

"When was she here?" Luc probed.

"Last weekend. When you and your sister were with Grandma."

"*Why* did you have her over here?"

"Because I like her. I like her a lot. She's a really nice person. And very pretty."

"Prettier than Mommy?" Luc demanded.

"No. No, of course not prettier than Mommy!"

"Well, why were her earrings off?" Luc demanded again. There were a few moments of silence. Papa was charting his response. I was very curious about what he would say and even in my embarrassment of what his answer might be, I remember hanging on his every word as I snooped through the wall.

"If you're going to make me spell it out for you Luc . . . we had sex. Next to the fireplace." I couldn't hear Luc's voice anymore. I think he was too shocked by my father's bluntness to speak. He was probably very embarrassed too.

"Is there anything else you want to know?" Papa inquired.

"Yes. *Why* did you do that?" Luc said.

"Why? Because I'm lonely. That's why."

"But you have *us*."

"That's not the same, Luc. That's just not the same. I need companionship."

I resented that Papa was pursuing companionship so soon, and I didn't think I would feel sorry if he actually got hurt in his endeavors, but I ended up coming to his pity party anyway. He looked like a cheerless little boy when Tracey, mystery woman from Los Angeles, dumped him. Tracey was an aspiring actress originally from Wichita, Kansas, who had found her way to Silver Lake in California with big dreams. She struggled tremendously in her film career and from what Papa told us was barely able to afford her tiny studio apartment off Sunset Boulevard.

When she dumped him, Papa cried. He looked so pathetic that it made me sad. As angry as he made me sometimes, I didn't want him to cry. His tears made me feel weak. I needed him to be strong.

"What should I do?" he asked me, thinking that I had the ability to provide smart counsel. "Should I try to get her back?"

I didn't want him to love anyone other than Mommy and furthermore, I didn't want to be his relationship shrink. I was uncomfortable with the position that he was putting me in, but I felt so sorry for him that I had to try to help him in the best way that I could.

"How do you feel about her?" I said.

"I'm in love with her," he replied.

"But you haven't known her that long. Mommy's only been dead for six months."

"Six months is a very long time," he said. I shrugged. How could I argue with how he experienced time? To me, six months seemed to be very little time when he was with Mommy for seventeen years. When I asked Grandma about it, she defended Papa by saying that a man could never go as long without a woman as a woman could go without a man.

"Does Tracey love you?" I asked Papa.

"I don't know."

"Did you tell her you love her?"

"Yes."

"And did she say she loves you back?"

"No. She didn't."

"So then forget about her, Papa. She clearly doesn't love you. You have to move on now. You'll find someone else. Someone who loves you too."

"Thank you," he said, smiling at me. "You give good advice. Your mom gave good advice too. I'm glad you are taking her place. When I hear your perspective on things, I feel much calmer."

"Okay. That's good I guess."

"So, what's new with you? Who are you spending your time with these days? Who are you hanging around with?"

"Nicole and the crew," I laughed.

"Nicole," he repeated, shaking his head. "Watch out for that girl. You know that I don't trust her."

"I know. But she's alright . . . you don't have to worry about it."

"Okay," he said. "You have to make your own decisions.

You're growing up now and you can pick your own friends. But be careful. I don't like that Nicole."

He nodded as if to agree with himself. His sad look returned. His little boy look. He traveled somewhere far away from me, far away from Nicole and not trusting her.

He was depressed for weeks over Tracey, and I worried about him. I didn't like him to be depressed, although he was nicer to me when he felt low. He picked on me less about mundane things and was more welcome to my advice.

I found him in his library before dinner time playing his guitar. He'd been singing the song *"Angie"* lately and I wondered if when he played it he was thinking about Tracey or Mommy or maybe both. When he sang that he saw Angie's eyes everywhere whose eyes was he seeing? I wanted them to be Mommy's.

He showed me pictures of Tracey. She had long, dark hair like Mommy once had and an attractive face. She *was* indeed very pretty, but she wore too much makeup. I told Papa that I thought so. He shrugged his shoulders. "I didn't mind."

He cooked me and Luc dinner during those weeks that he came home early from work. His cooking was much better than the take-out that we ordered when he was not around. The three of us sat at the wooden kitchen table, talking and laughing, Mommy's designated seat empty. We were a smaller family, but we were still a family. We were flawed, but still a family.

CHAPTER TWENTY-ONE

NICOLE WAS THE FIRST GIRL that rocked my world. She lived in a town called Port Washington, just a few miles north of Roslyn. A group of my friends hung out with a group of hers. We met in the tenth grade at a party and quickly became inseparable.

Nicole wasn't an honors student like I was. She faithfully failed math and barely floated in any other academic subject but for English classes where she got As. She wrote remarkable poetry and always analyzed literature brilliantly.

I didn't share my insight with her, but I always thought that she sabotaged her overall performance in school to get back at her nutty mother, Margaret. Margaret had no sense of boundaries. She nagged Nicole to such an extent that Nicole's whole life became a rebellion against her. Nicole refused to do anything that would make Margaret happy and since Margaret's biggest wish was for her to excel academically, she decided she'd might as well make school her very lowest priority. She cared much more for getting drunk, high, and in trouble.

Nicole only saw Margaret when the court said she had to. I know she felt vindicated that even the law conceded that she was best living with her father, Zachary, a mild mannered, passive sort of guy who somehow got looped into having four daughters with a control freak like Margaret.

Each time Margaret came to visit Nicole on her visitation

hours, Nicole got totally stoned before she arrived. Getting high was the only way Nicole could stomach Margaret's pesky, whiny voice drilling her on what proper etiquette was and what it meant to be a respectable person.

From her stellar modeling, I learned that Papa was also much easier to deal with if I was high. I got paranoid sometimes that he suspected something, but he never said a word.

Nicole came over from Port Washington after school. I picked her up in Mommy's Peugeot, which never officially became mine until I obtained a driver's license when I turned seventeen. My house on Hickory Hill felt palatial to her in comparison to the tiny, depressing apartment that she shared with Zachary. That apartment's living room had a fold-up table and several dingy chairs. There was a cut-rate couch, and no paintings or family photographs on the wall. All that was ever in the refrigerator was turkey, Hellmann's Mayonnaise, kaiser rolls, and a huge jar of Spanish olives. Zachary's room evoked a cheap motel-room feel. It had a worn-down dresser and bed. Its sparseness said that it was not for keeps, that it was just a place of transition. Nicole's room was the only room in the apartment that had any life to it. Her walls were papered with colorful tapestries that she bought at Grateful Dead Shows.

Zachary, like Papa, worked late in the city. After work, he was often on dates, searching for a new wife. He wanted to meet a woman who would bring him back some semblance of a home.

CHAPTER TWENTY-TWO

PAPA WAS WORKING a double shift at the restaurant, which would bring him home close to midnight. Luc was at a friend's house and was scheduled to be home by eight. I needed to be there when he got home. He was not to come home to an empty house, and I was appointed by Papa to the role of babysitter, much to my chagrin.

Nicole was getting high with her pot dealer Jon in the den. It bothered me to no end that she always needed to be high; I feared that she'd go down a shady road with harder drugs and never return.

I was drawn to the frailty that lay beneath her dangerous edge. Worrying about her destiny was some sort of mission that I was on; I had no idea what motivated me, just that I was pushed by some force that had a dark and cryptic power. There was no conscious awareness that my rescue fantasies were to avoid addressing my own pain. I lived with the compulsion to change her into the healthy person I thought that she should be.

I cooked her dinner and sometimes did the homework that lay untouched in her book bag. I played with her hair as she fell into a nap. I watched out for her daily with a care for her happiness that exceeded care for my own. Loving her made me feel better; it kept me from entering the menacing void of loss.

Her slightest sign of rejection could quickly dismantle me,

send me into a frightening tailspin. I did not know who I was without her approval or without her need for me. If she didn't need me, I had no purpose. So I made sure that she did.

Sometimes I thought that all girls secretly liked girls in the way that I did. Other times I felt perverted, sick for the places I traveled in my fantasy world. I tried to push away my feelings but could not. Trying to will my desire away just intensified it.

Nicole knew of my attraction to her; I was sure of it just by the look in her eyes. It was an unspoken truth that we shared; at moments I thought it was mutual, at other moments I had doubts. Thus I was the sicker one, the more deranged of the two of us.

I was too scared to ask her what she felt. Discussing it would make it too real. Acknowledging it verbally, in the open space, would give her the chance to reject me. If what went on remained unspoken about, we could live in a lie and I wouldn't have to lose her if she didn't feel the same. There were two planes of existence that I lived on. The real one and the one that I acted through to keep things safe.

"Hey you," she called at the door of my bedroom as I finished up a math problem set.

"Hey what?"

"You still doing homework, nerd?" she laughed.

"Almost done. Why?"

"Come downstairs and smoke a bowl with us."

I opened the door of my room and let her in. Her eyes

were glassy, her pupils contracted. She smelled like patchouli oil and the aftermath of a Newport cigarette.

"Is Jon still downstairs?"

"Yeah. He's in the den . . . packing a bowl that I hope you'll smoke with us."

I rolled my eyes at her.

"What?" she asked, innocuously. She knew I didn't like him, that he was crawling under my skin.

"I just think he's a creep."

"You think *all* guys are creeps."

"Yeah, but Jon, in particular, is a serious creep. Can't you ask him to leave already? You've been down there with him for hours."

"In a little while. Come smoke one bowl with us, and I'll tell him that you want me all to yourself." She winked at me, a kittenish look in her eyes. I followed her down to the den. Jon was sprawled out lackadaisically on the curvy, leather couch, a Ziploc bag of weed resting on the coffee table. The weed was forest green with flares of orange. Its potent smell filled the room.

"This bud is amazing," Nicole said. "Really." I nodded as she took the bowl that Jon packed off the table and lit it, taking a deep drag, blowing a clear, lengthy line of smoke through the room. She passed the bowl to me, laughing, reclining a bit on the couch, coughing.

Jon knew that I couldn't stand him. When he finally said goodbye, Nicole walked him out to his car, a beat up white Datsun that reeked of cigarettes. I *was* relieved to have her all to myself; she was different around others. There were different Nicoles. I suppose that there are different versions of everyone, but Nicole's various selves fascinated me. She changed to suit the situation she was in with incredible aptitude.

Around our peers, she lacked the warmth and grittiness that she revealed to me in private. I often felt like our closeness was some sort of a secret, not to be divulged, especially to other girls. I waited for the times it was just us, the times I felt like she was real.

Her eyes were green and captivating and her wavy black hair swept against her shoulder blades in curves. I loved to look at her. And I loved to read the entries of her "Nothing Book," a plain unadorned journal with quotes and poems that she either wrote herself or collected from varied sources. The poem that became my favorite was called "Comes the Dawn." There was a compelling force about it that resonated with me, and I repeated its words sometimes to myself for strength. It spoke of the importance of embracing loss and learning to depend on oneself.

"What time is Luc getting home tonight?" Nicole asked.

"Around eight."

"It's six," she said. "Want to take a spin?"

I knew it was not smart to drive when I was high but an instinct assured me that this was not a moment to miss, that all would be fine.

"Where do you want to go?" I asked her.

"Just around," she smiled.

"Just around," I laughed. "Okay."

She sat in the passenger seat of Mommy's Peugeot, hugging her knees. She wore tan Birkenstocks, ripped jeans, and a Grateful Dead T-shirt. The soles of her feet were pressed up against the dashboard. The scent of her patchouli oil flooded the car.

"Don't sit like that Nicole. If I stop short, your bones will break," I scolded at her playfully. She shrugged, paying my worries no mind, slipping a Dead tape from her knapsack into the tape deck. The song was "Scarlet Begonias."

She danced in her seat, carefree. When I was with her there was more than my sadness, the sorrow so real sometimes when I was alone. She had the free spirit that was trapped somewhere inside me, still afraid to come out.

We drove aimlessly around the windy roads of Roslyn Estates. The destination was trivial. What was important was that we were together, breaking the rules. There was no one keeping tabs on us, but we were keeping tabs on each other.

CHAPTER TWENTY-THREE

WE GOT HIGH in the car and came straight to the Ground Round, our favorite haunt, to binge on our favorite munchies: chicken fingers, fries, and garden salads with creamy peppercorn dressing. Jenny was our waitress; she was a friendly fixture of the Ground Round.

"So," Nicole said with a naughty expression on her face. "Donald Trump's wedding is tonight. To Marla Maples."

I shrugged, unsure of what significance it could possibly have to us, teenagers on Long Island.

"We're going," she said as I looked up.

"What are you talking about?"

"We're crashing it."

I laughed at her, bemused, realizing finally that she was not joking around at all.

"You're out of your mind," I giggled. "We're not crashing it."

We were in my bedroom not long after. As she tried on my strapless bras and black tie dresses, I called Papa at work, stealthily admiring her topless from the corner of my eye as I waited on hold for him to come to the phone.

"Yes, doll," Papa finally said. By the tone of his voice, I could tell he was in a good mood . . . on the light side of the moon.

"This is a new development, but Heather Feldman's father does business with Donald Trump, and he got comp tickets to Trump's wedding tonight at the Plaza Hotel and Heather invited me to come."

"Really?" Papa said. "That's incredible! Well I wouldn't want you to miss that. Do you have something to wear?"

"Yeah, a bunch of sweet sixteen dresses to pick from."

"Go ahead then! How will you get home?"

"Heather's dad will drive us home, but I'll crash at

Heather's tonight and just go to school with her in the morning. Luc said he could sleep at Andy's house."

"Okay, doll. Have Luc call me later to check in."

"Thanks Papa!"

Nicole was a little shorter than me, a little heavier as well, but our bodies pretty much fit into the same size dresses anyway. We both had small breasts and athletic builds. Both of the dresses we decided upon were black. Nicole did my makeup since I didn't have any, and didn't know how to apply it either.

What fascinated me was her insistence that we would get in, her absolute determination to succeed on this mission; she was so settled on getting through the doors of the Plaza that when we finally were stopped for our names after strolling past roaring crowds, and live newscasters asking celebrities for autographs, Nicole had actually brainwashed herself into believing we were invited to the wedding.

"I don't see your name on this list, ma'am," the security officer reiterated as I stood there, my heart thumping.

"Excuse me," Nicole barked. "My father is a long time associate of Trump. James Witherspoon is his name. My name is Randy Witherspoon and this lady with me is my guest." Her face was inflamed, and this I think was when I became aware of the fact that Nicole could convince herself of just about any storyline she wanted and would get irate at anyone who contradicted it.

I was unnerved by both her and the situation, not wanting to get arrested. She was enjoying it. She'd already spent the night in juvenile jail once when Margaret had her arrested for hitting her. She was also chased by the police for robbing a bagel store in the middle of the night with a bunch of friends from her school and writing in lipstick on the glass window of the storefront, "Sorry guys, no more bagels!"

"C'mon Nicole," I whispered. "We're not getting in here. I really don't want to end up in jail. My father will murder me."

She finally gave in and we slunk out in front of the crowd and news crews. We were jeered and booed at when we were thrown out.

Once back on fifty-ninth street, the south border of Central Park, Nicole informed me, as if I was on planet Earth simply to obey her commands, that we were not giving up yet—we would sneak through another entrance of the hotel to get to Trump's wedding bash anyhow.

Because we looked so stylish, they let us in at the entrance of the Edwardian Room where a medical conventional was being hosted for NYU med students. Nicole insisted that we check our coats; I was wearing Mommy's long, black, elegant Perry Ellis and she was wearing another fancy dress coat of Mommy's that she borrowed from the foyer closet. We ventured into a room with a large buffet dinner, found a small table for two, and headed to the buffet and bar to help ourselves. We were eating Italian food and sipping white wine for several minutes when Nicole needed to get the Newports that she left in her coat to go outside for a smoke.

"Left my butts in your coat," she said. "Be right back." I sat and waited for her for what seemed like a very long time.

At last, when she didn't return, I ventured out to the coat room and saw her arguing with security, insisting that she was a med student and not some sixteen-year-old party crasher. When security spotted me, instantly picking up that I too was involved in this preposterous fiasco, he said, "You two are *losers*. Now get the hell out of here before I call the cops and report you for trespassing!"

Once back on the street, Nicole was bitter, a pout on her gypsy face and a Newport already lit to soothe her nerves. "Nicole . . . clearly we've failed here," I said. "So let's just go home. There's a 10:20 train. I want to get on it."

"Baby," she said. "The night is young. It's not even ten. We're doing no such thing."

I conceded finally to take a cab with her to Tavern on the Green where we'd use the fake ID cards made by a laminating machine in this guy named John Busby's basement.

As this venture did not involve party crashing, we didn't exactly arouse the same level of suspicion, although we still got a look here and there as we were checking our coats. In a suave upstairs cocktail lounge we were approached by two men in their forties. They bought us drinks so we didn't have to show our IDs. We were already a little tipsy. One of the men said, "Would you ladies like to see New York City from a helicopter?"

Nicole's eyes lit up instantly. I pinched her hard under the table, saying *"no fucking way"* under my breath. She nudged me back to indicate, *yes*, pinching me even harder as retribution.

If ever there was a moment to assert myself this was it.

"No, thank you," I said to the men as Nicole glared at me. Who was I to rain on her parade?

"We'll, we'd like to see you ladies again," the men said. "Here's a little gift."

The slimier looking of the two wrote his phone number on a ten dollar bill that he'd removed from his wallet. He also handed us a joint. Nicole and I smoked it in Central Park a few minutes later.

We made a serious pact the next morning that none of our friends would find out that we got thrown out of Trump's wedding. We decided to lie, and tell made-up stories of conversations we had with all of the movie stars we encountered. So as far everyone knew, we had successfully crashed Trump's wedding.

One year later

CHAPTER TWENTY-FOUR

IT WAS THE DAY of Senior Prom. Papa drove me to the hair salon, videotaping me as I went inside.

"I'm very proud of you, doll," he said. "You look beautiful today."

When we got home, I put on the long black dress that he bought me at Bloomingdale's. He waited for me at the bottom of the stairs in the foyer when I came down in my dress, ready to meet my friends and their parents on our front lawn.

"You're embarrassing me," I laughed as he taped me.

"One day you'll watch this and you'll appreciate it. You'll want to remember me embarrassing you."

"Okay," I said. He followed me as I walked clumsily on my high heels out to the lawn where everyone was waiting, eating appetizers, and drinking from small, plastic glasses of champagne that he prepared.

Nicole was coming to the prom with us because a guy named Kevin that we hung out with asked her. While I was happy that she'd be there, I was jealous that Kevin could take her, instead of me . . . alone with my jealousy. I couldn't tell anyone, even the people that I loved so much that were everywhere around me. My date, Victor, a friend from my eleventh-grade history class, put on my corsage as I looked around for Nicole and Kevin, wondering why they were late.

Kevin's Bronco finally pulled into the driveway. He got out first to open the passenger seat for Nicole, helping her out. I winced as I saw him hold her hand as she stepped to the ground in her dress. He was stealing her from me without even realizing it.

Papa was entertaining everyone. He walked around with the video camera asking my friends questions about themselves and complimenting everyone on their outfits. Luc kept jumping in front of the video camera during Papa's interviews and telling jokes.

Papa told me that Victor and I looked good together.

"You should marry him one day," he whispered to me. "He's a very nice boy."

"No," I said, playfully pushing his arm. "I won't." He pulled me toward him and kissed me on the top of my head. I wondered if he knew how I felt about Nicole, if he would be angry at me if I were honest with him, or if he'd say it was okay. Sometimes I thought I could tell him, that he wouldn't judge me, that he'd love me anyway, but I couldn't bring myself to do it . . . just in case . . . just in case it would make him love me any less.

CHAPTER TWENTY-FIVE

PAPA DECIDED TO SELL our house in Roslyn. He and his girl-friend Mai would be taking Luc to Florida when I went to college, after the summer, the fall of 1994.

I didn't want them to move. I would miss the house that still held traces of Mommy, miss being able to come home to the place I knew as home. Luc didn't want to go either and start a life in a totally strange place with none of his friends and nothing familiar. Papa didn't listen. He said he couldn't stay for us.

"I can't live in New York anymore," he said. "The stress of working in New York City will kill me. I need an easier life."

Mai had lived around the world. She was originally from

Vietnam and had traveled extensively through Europe, South America, and Asia. She spoke seven languages fluently.

She came on the scene just a few months after Tracey dumped Papa, still less than a year after my Mommy's death and was my archenemy for several reasons. At first it was simply because she had buck teeth, a thick accent, and wore too much makeup. My grievances became far more serious when she started sleeping in my parents's bed after a very short period of dating Papa. While it was Papa's mistake, I punished Mai instead with nasty backtalk, dirty looks, and an overall reticence to warm my heart to her. I didn't accept any of the invitations that she extended to me to spend time with her. I kept my distance even in the moments when my conscience told me that she cared for me and wanted the best for me. Something visceral inside me made me reject her . . . if I really allowed myself to like her, I'd be betraying my mother.

"She's not going anywhere," Papa said to me whenever I pleaded with him to dump her. "So you better get used to her."

"Well, I'll *never* get used to her."

"Suit yourself. You always made things much harder for yourself than they had to be. She's perfectly nice to you."

"No she's not. She wishes I wasn't around and that she could have you all to herself."

"That's not true. She's good to you."

"She's not."

"You'd hate anyone that I was with."

"I don't think so."

"You'd hate anyone that wasn't your mother."

He was quite likely right, and I did little to smooth the pathway for him to invite another strong-minded female into our family. In fact, I got a reckless thrill out of fighting with her, of wedging my father between us. I enjoyed each moment of antagonizing her.

CHAPTER TWENTY-SIX

IN AUGUST OF 1994, Mai brought Luc to Florida to get him ready for high school. Papa stayed with me until it was time to take me to college orientation. For a week, he packed and got ready to close up the house while I said my final good-byes to all my friends. I remember my last moments in the house. I wanted to cling to what I knew and felt powerless against the impending change, unable to stop the onward flow of life. Time had an alarming pull and while I was excited to be a college student, I feared the journey ahead.

Most of the furniture was already gone. It was on a trailer on its way down south. The house was vacant and hushed. I wanted to hide in the closet of my bedroom as I did as a little girl when I wanted to be alone, putting blankets on the floor and wrapping myself inside of them with the small closet light on so that the closet would not be totally dark when I shut the door.

I was in my parents's room when Papa found me and

told me it was finally time to go. It was the moment I'd been dreading for months.

"Come on, doll. It's time."

"Just a little while longer," I said.

"Okay," he said, sitting next to me on the bed which he was selling to the new people that would live in our house. They had no rights to my house. I hated them without ever having met them. They were imposters.

"What if Mommy's ghost stays here when we go? What if she's trapped here?" I asked.

"I'm sure she won't be trapped here. I'm sure she'll follow you to school to watch over you. Or down to Florida to watch over me and Luc."

"I hope so."

"Everything will be okay, doll. It's a new life you're starting. College will be so exciting. You'll get involved in your life there and you'll forget about all this. You'll do a lot of growing."

"Do you promise that I'll be okay there, alone?"

"I promise," he said. "And you can come home and visit anytime. I'll buy you as many plane tickets as you'd like."

But it was not my home. Mai felt more threatening to me when she was no longer a guest in my house, and I was one in hers. "This is not your Roslyn house anymore," she said to me on one of my visits to Florida, aggravated by my sloppiness around the house. I only heard suggestion in her words: "This is not your mother's house. *I* am the important woman of this house now."

CHAPTER TWENTY-SEVEN

NICOLE ENDED UP graduating high school, despite my looming fears that she would not, that somehow she'd miss the boat and get left behind. She certainly wasn't headed to the Ivy League, but she was headed somewhere decent, which I was glad for.

I spent most of my freshman year daydreaming about her, wondering exactly where she was and who she was with in the town where she was at school.

She'd tell me on the phone about boys that she slept with. None of them sounded special to her; I feared that this could change any instant, never voicing my fears to her or to anyone.

She had a cousin who went to Cornell who decided to sublet her room for the summer. During the summer that preceded my sophomore year of college, we both lived in Ithaca, New York. In retrospect it was the summer where our bond was broken and when I started to become myself.

There was this swimming hole we went to called Six Mile Creek, a few miles from the Cornell campus. People sunbathed nude there. Nineties renditions of Sixties hippies brought their guitars and serenaded everyone throughout the day. Everyone drank beer and passed around joints. It was a hidden little utopia in the Ithaca woods.

Nicole loved to cliff jump. Each time she called my name

from a rock's jagged edge, my fatalistic imagination ran wild and I thought she'd never come up from the water. She always did. She emerged like a mermaid and came to lie next to me in the sun on the flat rocks.

We lay so close sometimes, tickling and caressing each other's skin, our lips nearly touching. I felt like if I kissed her she wouldn't stop me, but I just couldn't muster the nerve.

"We'll always be together, you and I," she said to me one day as I looked at the lake. The sun was setting. Her words did not comfort me; instead I was overwhelmed with pain. I must have known that it wasn't true, that it was quite the opposite.

It was not long after that moment at the lake when she said, "Sometimes I want to sleep with you. But other times I don't." We were on the roof of her cousin's house that looked upon the mountains. The sky was a deep blue and Nicole's boom box was playing a Grateful Dead bootleg. It was a conversation that always stayed etched inside me, a pivotal moment of my life that made others dull in comparison.

"Why? Why not those other times?" I said, hanging on her every word.

"Because I know it would change everything."

I wanted the change and she did not. That's how we differed and that difference was what charted our dissimilar courses in life.

CHAPTER TWENTY-EIGHT

SHE SAID THAT it was all in my mind and that nothing had changed. I tried to be convinced by her words but I knew they were lies. Something had changed since she met Sam.

I'd seen boys fall for her, but I'd never seen her fall back: madly in love. Totally taken by someone. So much of the function I'd filled, the noteworthy amount of attention that I always gave to her felt useless because the attention was coming from somewhere else. I felt like a source of something that she no longer needed. It hurts any girl when she loses her best friend to a boyfriend. My hurt was compounded by the fact that I loved her. The way she acted when she met Sam told me that any curiosity she'd felt about me was meaningless in the face of the force field of her passion for him.

"Hey," she said, standing at the door of my room. I'd waited for her for hours the night before. She said she'd be coming over, but never showed up. It was one P.M. the next afternoon. She'd been with Sam, and I'd cried through most of the night.

"Hey."

"What's wrong with you?" she asked.

"Nothing"

"C'mon. What's going on?"

"Nothing."

"Ha-ha. Tell me what's going on."

"I'm jealous," I said. "That you were with Sam."

"Okay. You're jealous. Because you don't have anyone. That's normal."

"No. I'm not jealous that you were with him. I'm jealous that he was with you. And I know you know what I mean."

She averted her eyes from me and fumbled with the bracelet on her wrist.

"I'm attracted to you," I continued. "I love you. I want to be with you: your girlfriend."

"No," she said, shaking her head. "That can't happen. That won't happen."

"Why?"

"Because you're my best friend."

"So, if I wasn't your best friend, it could happen?"

"No," she said. "It's not that . . . I'm not gay," she said.

"I don't know if I am either . . . but I love you."

"Well, I don't love you like that. And I never will."

I bit hard down on my lip and an unfamiliar coldness crept over me. I wanted her to leave, to disappear. I chose the less painful of two difficult choices: keeping her in my life or letting her go. To shut her out was to live with her ghost, but it was to be truthful to myself and to give myself a chance to grow. If I hadn't drawn the line, I know she wouldn't have. I would have kept on loving her and she would have kept letting me.

CHAPTER TWENTY-NINE

I HAD NEVER FELT so lost and alone. Sometimes I felt like I was nearing the edge of a cliff. Panic became such a part of my everyday life that I was waiting for some ultimate crash. I was sure that the bottom would fall out from under me, and I didn't know where to run since I was running from nothing but my own thoughts.

I became anxious over seemingly trivial things: an exam, ordering dinner, having a conversation with a professor. When the calm moments arrived, I hoped they would stay, but I could not hold onto them. They were fleeting, which created even more anticipation. This was the time that I began wandering, moving from location to location, scene to scene, an observer, moreover: a ghost. I was watching everyone else's world. Moving around helped me cope with the way that my thoughts would race. It was staying still that was troublesome. Falling asleep had begun to haunt me. My fear about going to bed started when the sun started going down . . . nighttime was a prison, my bed the jail cell. After a night of remaining wide awake, I was relieved when morning came. Daylight was safer, more hopeful. People were out and about . . . alive. At night it didn't just feel like everyone was asleep; it felt like they were dead and that I was the only one left living in the world.

It was four in the morning, and I'd been up for four nights in a row without a second of sleep. No matter how hard I tried to relax, I could not stop my thoughts from racing. I had a memory that hadn't come to me in years. It was of Mommy the night she died. Ruthie, the Jamaican Hospice nurse, was holding my hand, urging me to recite my final goodbye. The pale, yellow terrycloth cap on Mommy's head. Her bluish lips. The brown, rectangular oxygen tank on the floor next to her bedside. Mommy gasping for air. The terse breaths. The fear in her eyes when she opened them. She'd wanted to communicate something to me but was unable to. . . .

I couldn't calm down no matter what I tried: meditating, praying, caressing myself gently as if I were my own child. My skin was covered in goose bumps, and I shook in bed under my covers. When I put my fingers against my earlobes, my heart was beating so loudly that it felt as if someone was chasing me up a stairwell.

The longer that I stayed up, the less my mind was able to rest. I was worried that I wouldn't be able to sleep again and that I might go insane from exhaustion. I considered checking into a hospital in the morning.

For months I'd been picturing an imaginary hospital, a place that I could go just as I was about to fall over that cliff . . . just as the bottom was about to fall out from under me. It was a place of safety where total strangers would care for me, and I wouldn't have to go through the shame of telling people just how shaky everything had become.

Before I left the house in the darkness to go walking through Ithaca, I called Papa in Florida. My clock read 4:27 A.M. Mai answered the phone.

"Hello," she said in her feminine whisper.

"Can I speak to my father?"

"He's asleep."

"I need to talk to him."

"This can't wait until the morning?"

"No. It can't wait. Wake him up."

Papa finally mumbled hello into the phone.

"Yes, doll," he said.

"I can't sleep, Papa. I've been up for almost four days."

"You'll get to sleep if you keep trying. When there's something on my mind I can't sleep either. It runs in the family."

"But I'm scared."

"Don't be scared. Maybe get up and do something for a while and then try again."

"I've tried that Papa. It doesn't work."

"Well I don't know what to tell you then, doll," he snapped. "It's the middle of the night, and I'm very tired. Let's talk some more in the morning, okay?"

"Okay," I conceded, putting down the phone.

It comforted me to think that Mommy would have stayed on the phone, or driven straight to Ithaca to visit me in my despair. There was no one else that I wanted to burden, to request that which would have been entirely acceptable to ask from her. *Please don't leave me until this nightmare is over. Please. Don't leave.*

Not even Papa.

I dressed warmly, piling several layers of clothing

beneath my down jacket and walked down Blair Street, up Cook Street, headed to Collegetown Avenue, the hub of Cornell University's college town.

No one was out. It was a desolate, dark little ghost town. I headed through the village of restaurants, convenience shops and nightlife bars toward campus grounds. The fact that I was the only one straying through campus in the dark made me feel freakish.

I walked briskly for miles without a specific destination, finally sitting for a while on the Suspension Bridge, world famous for suicide. I gazed into the void thinking how easy it would be to just die. A professor I recognized walked across the bridge, a five A.M. mug of coffee in hand.

"You alright?" he asked me uneasily when he reached where I was, midway across the bridge, which had high railings now, installed by Cornell to prevent future deaths.

"Yeah," I said, nodding. "I'm fine. I just couldn't sleep."

"Sometimes it's hard around here," he laughed. "Lots of school work that you're stressed over?"

"Yeah," I laughed. I was trying to display sanity through my eyes, while behind them questioning my good sense, wary of my own strength. My mask worked though; I had fooled another person by appearing composed.

"Well, take care," he said, leaving me there, continuing his walk. I watched him saunter away. I stayed for a while before I decided to go down into the gorge I had been looking at.

There was little ice on the trail heading downwards. My winter boots felt secure on the rock steps, heavy as horse hoofs. I braved the steep stairway that declined into the mystical abyss which was carved so perfectly into the world.

The sound of the gorge hit me before the sight. It was a peaceful murmur, a lulling voice, as if beckoning me somewhere invisible. As I neared the cavernous bottom, the view became more and more earth shattering. I smiled when I saw the clean, white, majestic torrent slamming against the rocks, and breathed the moist, cold air deep into my lungs. I exhaled it outward toward the leafless trees and watched it drift into ringlets of smoke.

I was relieved to be the only one there, to have the beauty all to myself. I found a dry place to sit on the black slate rocks that piled on top of one another. They eased gradually into the clear cold lake that the waterfall emptied itself into in an eternal flow.

I closed my eyes and focused on the murmur of the water hitting the rocks. When my eyes were closed, I felt totally invisible. My body could have faded away into the scenery, and I wouldn't have minded. My soul might not have lingered, but I didn't care. The way I was thinking was alarming . . . I hadn't thought like this before. It scared me to feel it would be okay to die at twenty years old.

My walk back up to level ground was exhausting. A dizzying headache pierced through my eyes. I looked around for the closest pay phone, finally stumbling into the Hillside Inn, a cheap motel on Stewart Avenue, which was not far from the West Campus gorge. The innkeeper on the night shift who was sitting at the front desk said that I could use the phone. I sequestered myself in the tiny booth and dialed the digits of my calling card and Papa's number. This time there was no answer at the house. The phone rang and rang but no one picked up.

"Fuck," I shouted out loud into the sealed booth, slamming down the phone. I wanted to crumple up like a piece of paper, taken for trash, thrown away. I walked farther away from campus then, away from my life of a college student, trekking to downtown Ithaca, where real people lived, not just students in a cushiony world. I walked out onto a highway route that led out of town, Route 96, wishing that it were an escape to another life where I wouldn't feel what I was feeling. Finally I sat down on the cold, grassy sidelines of the highway, watching tractor trailers go by. In my mind's eye, I jumped in front of each them as an ominous voice in my head spoke to me. *Jump. I dare you to jump. No one will miss you. There might be nothingness when you die and nothingness would be so much better than all of this.*

I kept my eyes shut, listening to the sound of passing trucks in the night, opening them only occasionally to see headlights which lit up the road flashing by me. I thought of Mommy again. In this flashback, she was healthy and vibrant. Her hair was its rich brown, long and flowing. Her eyes were bright and her cheeks a blush color. The image, so peaceful, kept fading in and out. It was like a dream that I was trying to hold onto when the alarm clock rang. I thought about what she would have said to me if she could see me at that moment on the side of the highway, so close to daybreak, wanting to die. She'd have told me to keep on living, to fight harder, not to give up, that sunlight was around the bend. There would be better days.

I lifted myself from the ground, starting my trek back to campus. I breathed deeply and repeated positive affirmations out loud. *You're going to be okay. You're going to survive.* Dawn was breaking and while it was a gray, wintry kind of light, I still felt some hope.

Entering the house quietly, I found my plastic bathroom bin and redid each of my evening rituals. I washed my face with tea tree oil soap and brushed my teeth rigorously with cinnamon toothpaste. I took a hot shower and rubbed lavender oil into my skin, put my flannel pajamas back on with a warm pair of socks. When I got back into bed, I tried to study, but the words in the textbook were drivel on the page. They roamed with my eyes.

I still couldn't sleep. Each moment when I almost lost consciousness, my body jerked up as if I were having a seizure. I pictured Mommy again, feeling solace, knowing it was time to go for help. Before I fell from the cliff. Before the bottom fell out.

CHAPTER THIRTY

THE WAIT AT CORNELL'S MENTAL HEALTH CLINIC was not long, but there were many more students there than I had anticipated. I was assigned to a psychiatrist named Trista, who introduced herself to me by her first name instead of

Doctor something or other. She called to mind Doctor Lowenstein in *The Prince of Tides*, even bearing some small resemblance to Barbra Streisand with the Roman nose and the regal, impressive office.

"How can I help you?" she asked me sincerely.

"I've been thinking lately that I really wouldn't mind dying . . . I'm scared."

I know she wished that she had the time to hear my story in depth—the specific events that brought me to this moment in her office. But it was clear to me that she was in over her head and only had time for the quick, formulaic, signifying words for a pharmacist on her prescription pad.

"You are very tired now. And very depressed," she said. "You need *sleep* more than anything. The less you sleep, the less clarity you have about anything. It is not your 'fault' that you haven't slept in four nights. You are being way too hard on yourself and should really stop that as it will not benefit you at all. Your brain is depleted of serotonin. We must get you sleeping again, and I know these prescriptions will do the trick. However, there is someone I want you to speak with. A bereavement specialist named Laure. She works with many students here who have lost parents and understands the specifics of that psychological experience. She's a remarkable person and right here at the clinic."

I was afraid that pills would alter my personality, make me feel like a stranger to myself.

"Nonsense," Trista said. "Medication will bring you back

to base level and will allow you to be productive again. Just last night you thought of jumping in front of trucks on route 96. You should not be thinking about dying now, but about living. You are so young."

"Will I still be creative if I take the medicine?" I asked. "Because I want to be a writer."

"More so. When the depression lifts, your writing will improve. I promise."

"Will medication make me happy?"

Trista sighed. She didn't want to lie to me, and I appreciated her honesty.

"Happiness takes very hard work, dear. Laure will help you more with that. The medicine will take the edge off and help you to function better. I'd like you to talk to Laure. More than once a week if need be."

I immediately took the Trazadone that Trista prescribed for sleep. They were magic yellow pills. I slept long and hard, savoring the ability to lose consciousness, which I'd always taken for granted before I could not sleep. I also began a low dosage of an SSRI. My panic gradually subsided, and I was able to resume my daily activities and function like I had before depression set in. While there was controversy on campus about whether taking medication was the right thing to do since so many students at Cornell were tossed Prozac and such to cope with their stress, I knew that it was the right choice for me. In fact, I think it saved my life. I've never regretted it, but sometimes I've wondered what would have happened to me had I refused the help.

Laure was Cornell University's on-site bereavement counselor. She began working with me in the fall of 1996. Her hair was whitish blond and the sunlight that poured through the oversize window of her office illuminated her aura. She was an extraordinarily gentle and compassionate woman, and I felt at ease in her presence. She listened to me and did not judge me. And she helped me to judge myself less harshly . . . to slow down the inner attack that went on inside me. To recognize, observe, and contemplate so many of the ways that I needlessly castigated myself. To love myself a bit more . . .

It became uncanny that Laure came into my life at the time she did. In fact, we were both shocked to realize that she was there to help me with more than the death of my mother and that another major loss was lurking closely in the wing.

CHAPTER THIRTY-ONE

MAI CALLED ME at college in January of 1997. It was a rarity for her to call me at all, so I was immediately panic stricken when I heard her voice.

"How are you?" I asked.

"I'm not so well. There's a problem here."

Initially, I thought that something had happened to Luc, that perhaps he'd been in a car accident.

"Daddy is losing all of his coordination," she said.

"Papa? How?"

"I'm not sure. He hasn't been able to put his shirts on right, or to tell the time on the digital clock in our room. Last week we were playing tennis, and he couldn't align the ball correctly with the racquet. He kept missing the balls as he swung at them."

"What do you think is wrong?"

"I have no idea. But I'm at the hospital now, in the waiting room. He's getting some tests done."

"Where's Luc?"

"He's at school. Your dad wanted him to go to school this morning even though he wanted to come to the hospital."

When I hung up the phone, my housemate Kimberly walked into my room. She'd overheard me on the phone.

"Are you okay?" she asked.

"I'm not sure."

"What's the matter?"

"My father is in the hospital; I just got a call from his girlfriend that he's losing his coordination."

"What's causing it?"

"They don't know yet . . . but they're doing a spinal tap now; she's going to call me when she knows something more."

"Don't assume anything. It could be absolutely nothing."

But I knew that it was not nothing. I knew it as if it had

already happened . . . the moment where I learned that my father was dying. The script would arrive with the day's mail. In the performance, I would be the daughter who learned that her father had very little time.

"I understand you're saying that you get these intuitions," Kimberly said when I described the sixth sense that I had about what was happening, "But I think you're getting ahead of yourself here."

"I don't think so Kimberly. I have a very bad feeling."

I called the house in Florida for hours. It was after nine in the evening when Luc finally called me.

"We just got back home from the hospital," he said.

"Okay. So what's going on?"

"Here's Papa," he said, putting Papa on the phone.

"Hi, doll," Papa said.

"What is going on? Please tell me."

"I would like you to come home and I can speak to you then."

"I'll come home, but please tell me what's wrong."

"No. I want to tell you and Luc together . . . it's very hard for me to say, so I only want to say it once."

"I can't handle waiting. I can deal with whatever you say now," I told him.

After all, I was sure that he was dying. I couldn't imagine any worse information than that. But he wouldn't tell me anything.

I booked my plane ticket for the next morning.

Luc was waiting for me at the terminal in Fort Meyers, Florida; I spotted him from the escalator as I rode my way down to baggage claim. He was just outside the terminal, smoking and pacing.

He was sixteen and in most ways seemed like your average teenage boy although there was this wisdom about him which also made him appear older than his years. He signaled, spotting me, smiling as I walked toward him. As he took my carry-on bag, I kissed his tanned cheek, and followed him out to his car which was in short-term parking. Papa's old Mercedes.

"How is Papa?" I asked.

"Different from anything you've seen. You better prepare yourself. He's changed a lot. Really fast. It's frightening."

"Is he dying?"

Luc nodded his head, and didn't fight back his tears.

"But you have no clue what's wrong?"

"None. No one will tell me anything."

"Strange. So strange."

"But we'll find out soon enough," Luc said bitterly, taking a Newport out of the half-empty pack on his dashboard and lighting it up. I didn't know what words of solace to offer him, wishing that I had some.

When we arrived home there were two cars in the driveway other than Papa's and Mai's: Grandma and Grandpa's green Buick, and an economy-size rental car that Uncle Benjamin rented at the airport in Fort Meyers when he flew in from Los Angeles earlier that evening.

The house was silent when we entered, even though I knew that everyone was there, in anticipation of us. It was the creepiest minute of my life. Luc and I walked up the staircase. Grandma and Grandpa sat next to each other on the living room couch, only inches away from one another. They shared the world so closely. Their inner worlds fused, forming one proverbial mind. They were each other's best advocate, and the sole model of enduring love in our family.

Aunt Karen had not come with Uncle Benjamin. She was in Los Angeles taking care of Cory, but she and Benjamin were splitting up, anyhow, after twelve years of marriage. We'd received the sad news recently.

Uncle Benjamin's eyes were strained. He was always on planes, in transit from one destination to another. It was typically for business, but tonight he was here because Papa was dying. It was clear to me that he'd already been told what was happening, as had Grandma and Grandpa and that they pitied me and Luc. They felt bad for what we were in line to hear.

I kissed Grandpa's whiskery face and shook his wrinkled hand. Grandma got up to kiss me. "Hi darling," she said, embracing me. She smelled like *White Diamonds,* her signature perfume.

"My niece," Uncle Benjamin smiled when he hugged me. "Almost a grown-up woman!"

I didn't know him well. I remembered him from the earlier years of my life when he and Aunt Karen lived near our Roslyn house in Sea Cliff, a town several miles away. On

Sundays we had family barbeques, and on holidays, holiday dinners. And there were those joyful weekends shared together at the Hamptons house. He and Karen moved to Los Angeles when I was eleven, and except for some short visits here and there, I hadn't seen much of him. He flew in for the Sweet Sixteen party that Papa threw me, but I was too occupied with my friends to pay much attention to him that day. I felt comfortable around him, though. He was a gentle and reasonable man. He had such a different personality than Papa, who was so erratic and hot-blooded.

"Where is Papa?" I asked. Grandma said he was in the master bedroom with Mai. I braved myself to walk in to see him. Luc and Uncle Benjamin followed me while Grandma and Grandpa stayed seated as they were on the living room couch.

Mai smiled at me gently when she saw me. She was not my enemy anymore. I felt no animosity toward her.

Papa was in bed, on top of the covers, perched up against several pillows. The sheets were part of the black-and-white checkered set that he had for years, from before Mommy died.

His eyes were sickly, crazed. When he first made eye contact with me it was as if he was possessed by something.

"Hi, doll," he said. "You're finally home. Thank you for coming so fast. It means a lot to me."

"I'm here now," I said. "Can you please tell us what is wrong?" I glanced at Luc who looked as expectant as I did.

Papa paused, buying time.

"Can I tell you in French?"

"I don't understand French," I said. "You know that."

"I'll translate what you say for her," Luc said, encouraging him. "What is it Papa?" he probed.

"It's called 'SIDA,'" Papa finally pronounced as I looked at Luc, anxiously waiting for his translation.

"AIDS," Luc whispered.

There *was* something worse than the fact that he was dying. He was dying from *AIDS*.

"How did you get this Papa?" I asked.

"I don't know, doll," Papa said. "I really don't know."

"Did you even know that you had HIV?"

"No. I had no idea. None at all."

"Daddy was as shocked as you are right now," Mai confirmed. "After all the tests—the spinal tap—when they finally came to us with these results, your father was completely shocked."

Her eyes were forthright and genuine.

"What about you Mai?" I said. "Are you sick too?"

"I haven't been tested yet," she said. "But I'm not worried . . . I think I'm okay."

"Why? *Why* would you think you're okay?"

"Because I feel perfectly healthy."

"But that means nothing with HIV . . . a person can feel perfectly healthy and still be a carrier."

"Well for now, I'll just have to pray for the best. Daddy needs me now, and I have to focus on him. Not me."

"Do you have any idea at all how you could have gotten this Papa?" Luc said. Papa looked contemplative.

"A few years ago, a friend of mine was dying. We got drunk one night and made a blood brother's pact."

"Did you know that he had AIDS?"

"Yes."

"Well, why would you have done that?" I demanded. "Didn't you know you could catch it like that?"

"I really didn't think I could, no. But there are two other things that I'm thinking about. . . . There was a car accident once on the Long Island Expressway that I stopped to help with. Maybe I got blood on me, and it was infected blood. I also cut myself in the kitchen once at work and needed a transfusion in the hospital, because I lost a lot of blood."

"But you're not sure which of these things it was?"

"No."

I was lost somewhere in my racing thoughts, trying to do the math, feeling like nothing added up.

"Kids," Papa said. "It is very important to never tell anyone what I have or how I died. Do you promise me that you won't?"

Luc and I both promised.

I knew he was concealing something. He didn't want to tell us how he really contracted it. While I knew he was lying, it didn't matter right then and there. Uncle Benjamin explained to me that the AIDS was full blown, in advanced stages. It could not be treated. Papa had PML which was a type of dementia. His mind would go first. Then all of his organs would shut down, one by one. He would not live longer than six months, if that.

Uncle Benjamin followed me out of the room, down the narrow corridor of the apartment to my room. I heard my grandparents's footsteps coming from the living room as I lay down on my bed and sobbed. I cried like I was five years old and could not get my way. Uncle Benjamin sat down on the bed next to me, rubbing my back and playing with my hair.

"Everything is going to be okay. I promise," he said.

"Why does it have to be the worst of the worst that he has . . . the worst disease that anyone can possibly get?"

"It's not the worst. That's just how the media spins it. AIDS is like any other terminal illness. It's the stigma about it that is making you feel this way. You need to get past the stigma because if you don't, this is going to be much more difficult to cope with. Many many people in this world have AIDS. It is nothing to be ashamed of. Don't be ashamed of your father. Don't judge him."

"I'm not judging him. I'm going to miss him."

"So am I," Uncle Benjamin said sadly. "I love him."

Grandma and Grandpa stood at the door of my room in silence, staring at me. When Uncle Benjamin left to go check on Luc, Grandma came to take his place next to me on my bed. Grandpa moved a bit further into my room, still standing poker faced near the door.

"You mustn't tell *anyone* about the AIDS," Grandma whispered to me. "It could ruin all of our lives."

She was bothering me. In fact, she was making me furious. She was thinking about image, appearances, how it
would all look. Her mentality irritated me tremendously. I
could not relate to it. Her concern for appearances was always something that I was aware of and always something
that got on my nerves. She'd pulled me over to the side many
times throughout my childhood and told me that family
business should stay within the family and that I should
never tell any of my friends anything personal that went on
in my house. Friends were not to be trusted . . . at the end of
the day, blood was thicker than water. These talks came
along with other types of talks such as the talks to remind me
that I was Jewish and needed to value my Judaism and the
talks where she insisted that I keep my room as clean and or-
ganized as possible. Her talks annoyed me because she was
trying to control me. My natural instinct about what to do
was so other to her advice.

I had no strength to retaliate while I knew that I could
nor would ever keep such a secret. There was no need to ag-
gravate her further, even though she was aggravating me.

When I collected myself a little, I went back to Papa's
room.

"Doll," Papa said. "Can I have a hug?"

I was ashamed of the thought that ran through my mind
when he asked me that question. I actually wondered whether
I could catch AIDS, knowing that no one ever got AIDS
from giving someone a hug or from any of the other forms
of contact I had with him. But there was this primal fear.

This voice in my head was speaking to me about the intima-
cies I had shared with him: the baths I'd taken in his Jacuzzi
tub, my swigs of his Listerine if the bottle in Luc's and my
bathroom was empty. I thought of how it was he who took
me to the emergency room a few years back when I cut my
hand open on New Year's Eve. I had been washing a wine
glass in the kitchen; it broke in my hand and when my hand
split open, I needed seventeen stitches. I wondered if there
could have been an open cut on him that touched any of my
blood. All these fears raced through my mind as I lay down
to hug him, appalled by my dumb thoughts, my blind fear, of
anyone's blind fear about AIDS.

"Of course you can have a hug," I said, crawling next to
him, wrapping my arms snugly around his body. He smelled
sickly. His face was pale and had thinned. His pupils were di-
lated. I pressed my cheek against his chest.

"Are you scared?" I asked him.

"No."

"Do you think you'll see Mommy, when you die?"

"I know that I will," he said. "In fact, I am sure of it."

"Do you still want to be cremated? You've always said
that you'd want that."

"Yes."

"I really don't want you to be."

"Well, I wouldn't do anything to hurt you, doll." He
paused.

"So you'll be buried?"

"Yes. If that's what you want."

"It is. Thank you."

I kissed him goodnight and went to the shower. There was a knock at the door shortly after.

"It's Mai. Can I come in?"

"Yes," I said.

"Are you all right?" she asked.

I watched her through the smoky glass of the shower pane. She sat down at the vanity table, placed her head in her hands. I could see that she was totally exhausted, physically and psychologically.

"Yes. But what about you, Mai? You *need* to get tested for HIV."

"I will," she said. "When the time is right."

"When will the time be right?" I asked.

"In a few weeks, maybe."

I regretted ever hating her, and prayed for the miracle that she'd be fine. She had to be a carrier, no matter what she speculated about being okay. She'd had numerous unprotected encounters with my father in the five years that she'd been with him. Only uncanny luck, or divine intervention would make her okay and I expected neither.

I asked Papa if he wanted me to drop out of school for the semester and live home.

"No. Please go back to Cornell and get good grades. That will make me the happiest." I was relieved to not have to stay there and watch him waste away. Luc had no choice since he was already there.

I went into his room the morning after we received the news. He was lying in bed watching cartoons, staring numbly at the television set. I crawled into bed with him, squeezing my body against him, feeling more like his younger sister than his older one of four years. I fell back asleep next to him. When I woke up again, nearly at noon, he was sleeping soundly next to me.

Papa, Uncle Benjamin, and Mai were at the lunch table. Grandma and Grandpa had headed back to the east coast of Florida where they lived. Mai had just made Papa a BLT sandwich and put the plate down in front of him. Papa tried picking the sandwich up, but he kept dropping it back onto the plate. Finally the entire sandwich fell apart.

"Hi, doll," he said then, noticing me in the room.

"How are you today? How is my girl? I couldn't ask for a better daughter in the world."

He stood up from the kitchen table. He had the same peculiar look in his eyes from the night before as he attempted to walk over to the sink.

"Remy, what do you want?" Mai said, anxiously. "Just tell me and I'll get it for you." In a premonition, I saw him falling hard against the ground.

"No. I can get it myself," he insisted, collapsing on his way to the sink. Mai screamed out as he fell to the floor. Uncle Benjamin lifted him up and carried him over to the couch.

"I think we should call an ambulance," he said.

Papa was hallucinating and babbling about whatever he saw. I waited on the couch with him and held his hand until the paramedics arrived. A few men strapped him onto a stretcher and brought him out to a miniature white truck. Uncle Benjamin rode with him to the hospital. Mai drove me and Luc who had woken up from the commotion.

Papa looked more at ease in his hospital bed. I couldn't stop crying, seeing this new version of him. He had been healthy, and suddenly out of nowhere he was an AIDS patient. He watched me as I cried.

"It isn't easy, is it?" he asked.

I could barely stand to look at him. I walked out of the room, down the hall to the waiting room. Sitting on the couch, I took a stack of magazines off the coffee table onto my lap, ripping each of them up methodically. The next time I looked up, Mai who sat down next to me and took the magazine I was ripping, easing it out of my hands. She cuddled me, rocking me back and forth. I let myself relax into her arms.

"Are you hungry?" she asked. I shrugged as she picked up all the ripped magazine pieces from the floor.

"We'll buy some more magazines for people in the gift shop," she said. "Luc wants to go to Applebee's across the street for some hamburgers. Do you want to come with us?"

"Okay," I said.

"So let's say goodbye to Daddy for now."

I knew I wasn't coming back.

"I'll buy you a lot of tickets to come see me, doll," Papa said when I walked back into his room to say my last goodbye.

I nodded my head agreeably, giving him no inclination

of my intentions. I wonder if he suspected them. I wonder if he knew that I didn't have the strength to return. "Okay, so I'll see you very soon," I said, knowing that I was lying, knowing that he'd understand my decision.

Luc brought me to the airport the next morning. My flight back to Ithaca was scheduled to leave at eleven. He'd already driven off when I noticed on the departure screen that the flight had been canceled and was rescheduled for the next day.

"What happened with my flight?" I probed a receptionist at the desk.

"It was rescheduled until tomorrow morning because of a mechanical problem with the plane."

"Please," I said, "Put me on another flight."

"There are no other flights to Ithaca, ma'am."

"Can I fly somewhere else and fly to Ithaca from there?"

"Let me check," she conceded, rustling her ponytail, smiling.

"I appreciate this," I said. "I really need to get back."

I kept remembering the moments before I'd come home. Going back there in my mind created a sense of relief. If I brought myself back to the time before the news, I could imagine a totally different unfolding of events. An unfolding where Papa would be able to live.

"Ma'am," the receptionist finally said as I looked up. I'd gone somewhere else. Back to the hospital room.

Isn't easy, is it?

"I can fly you out to Chicago and then route you to

Ithaca that way. It's out of the way, but if you really have to get back, this is the best I can do for you."

"I'll take it," I said, thanking her several times over. "I really appreciate your help."

CHAPTER THIRTY-ONE

I WATCHED PAPA die through Luc and Mai's descriptions over the phone. Grandma didn't want to tell me what things really looked like, but Luc and Mai did, even though I never probed too hard. I didn't ask them for the details they provided.

Luc took weeks off from high school because he was unable to concentrate on any of his work. His mind was on spending as much time with Papa as he could. He brought Papa's record player from the 1970s to the nursing home where Papa was relocated. (The hospital said they could do nothing for him that a nursing home couldn't do just as well or better.) Luc played him the music he loved . . . Billie Holiday, Nina Simone, The Stones. He was patient with him even when Papa's moods changed radically. Sometimes Papa drifted into a state of insanity and was filled with wrath for the world. At times he told Luc to get out of the room and that he didn't want to see him ever again. Luc left hesitantly, wanting to stay.

He was angry that I wouldn't come home. Nothing I said could change that.

Each night Mai spoke to me, telling me the events of the day with Papa at the nursing home, leaving out few gritty details. She spoke for long periods of time, without asking for a response. I know she just needed someone who would listen to her.

One night she told me that Papa had disappeared from his room. He was found nude, wandering aimlessly in an empty corridor with his arm still attached to the IV machine.

"Daddy got lost today," she said. "No one could find him."

It was a metaphor—each day his mind got more and more lost. Ultimately no one would know where it had gone, which begged the question for me of where minds went when they got lost. Where was the soul when the mind was just mumble-jumble madness?

I spoke to Papa each day when Mai put the phone up to his ear. I asked him questions or just listened to him ramble if he was incoherent. Sometimes he knew who I was and sometimes he didn't.

"I want to tell you about AIDS, doll," he said once, not finishing his thought.

"What? What do you want to tell me about AIDS?" I asked, but he started speaking gibberish again.

I asked Grandma if I made the wrong decision and whether if I should come back home to see him again. She was the only one that I asked because I knew she'd be the only one to tell me to stay where I was, to avoid the pain. She gave me the perfect license to hide that I was looking for.

"Don't come. It's bad here. It will do you no good to see this. It will not better you."

I wondered if that was the point. Was the point for me to be bettered or to be a support?

When Papa went blind, close to the end, Mai arranged for a spirit guide who was a Native American Indian healer to come to the nursing home. She claimed to help prepare Papa to go peacefully to the other world. Mai believed in reincarnation and was sure that in the afterlife, Papa would enter a new body.

"He is just so angry," she said. "Sometimes just furious. The healer is trying to help heal his anger, so that he doesn't enter a new body with all of this rage."

She slept at the nursing home most nights on a cot next to him, so that if he woke up he wouldn't be scared. She coaxed him on his journey to an unknown world.

Papa told Luc and Mai that he changed his mind about cremation: he wanted to be cremated and sprinkled in the forests of Font D'Vreau where he played as a little boy.

"It's what he wants," Luc snapped at me on the phone.

"But he promised me that he wouldn't do it," I said. "He and I had an agreement."

"Well, why should it be up to you?"

"It's not up to me. It's just what Papa agreed to when I spoke to him about it."

"Well, he's changed his mind," Luc hissed.

"You can't possibly be serious. Now that he is completely delirious, you are going to listen to him? When he was still half sane, he promised me that he'd be buried."

"You're not even here."

"I may not be there, but I am just as much his child as you are and the decision is just as much mine. So there needs to be a compromise."

When our fighting subsided, Papa on his death bed, we agreed to bury him next to Mommy in Queens, New York, in Grandma's family plot. The problem was that Grandma and Grandpa refused us, not willing to grant our wish or at the very least explain their reasoning.

"Why?" each of us demanded to know.

"Because he doesn't belong there."

"Our father doesn't belong next to our mother?"

"Your father doesn't belong in the family plot. Besides, he's not Jewish," Grandma said.

"He *is* Jewish. He legally converted to Judaism."

"He doesn't belong there," Grandpa said, adamantly. There was no room for negotiation.

Uncle Benjamin came up with a different solution. We would bury Papa in Font D'Vreau near the forests where he played as a little boy. We would travel there when he died, back to where his family of origin would await us and the casket. We would bring him back home. . . .

CHAPTER THIRTY-TWO

"*NOUS ARRIVONS À PARIS À HUITE HEURS DU MATIN,*" the stewardess announced through the loudspeaker.

I stretched and opened my eyes, waking from the plane's simulated night. The sun was rising over Paris, and I watched the expanse of clouds from my window seat as we moved miles through the sky. I was daydreaming of nightmares that were real to me: the funeral service in Florida. Mai's white dress (Papa wanted his funeral to be a party), the colored helium balloons that filled the room. *"Dust in the Wind"* playing on Luc's boom box. Uncle Benjamin's eulogy about the poor country boy who came to America in '74 and became a success. The successful French chef in the cherry-wood casket, draped with the French flag. Papa.

"He loved his homeland," Uncle Benjamin said to the crowded room. My eulogy, in which I thanked Papa for encouraging me to always be myself, never to compromise who I was. The cherry-wood coffin being wheeled onto the plane when our flight to Paris was about to leave Miami, Florida, the evening before.

"That's Remy," Uncle Benjamin had said, pointing to the men wheeling it. I'd turned my eyes to look out the window, for a second believing that Papa was there, alive on the runway, soon seeing the coffin rolled onto the bottom of the plane to ride with the luggage.

It was my first time flying to France without him, and

the first time I walked numbly through de Gaulle airport. The secondhand cigarette smoke was making me cough and Papa was not there, offering to buy me *café au lait* and *croissants au chocolate*. I was looking around the terminal for him, despite what I knew about death, still expecting that he could turn any corner any instant.

"Doll," I heard him say. *"Even though you're tired, it's best to try to stay awake for the day and then sleep well at night. That's the way to beat jet lag. Trust me."*

"But I'm tired Papa. I can't stay up."

"If you sleep now, you'll be up all night and then you'll never get on track."

"I need to sleep."

"Okay. Okay."

My family walked through customs to baggage claim in an exhausted, silent procession, like somber cars on the way to a gravesite. Luc lit a Newport. I was daydreaming again. Papa and I were at a café together, somewhere in the Latin Quarter. I was drinking Orangina in a tall, thin glass with crushed ice. Papa was drinking red wine. We were talking, laughing, and observing the passersby.

"You should live here in Paris one day, doll," he said. "I would pay for you to have an apartment here. You should get to know French culture."

"Really?"

"Yes."

We headed first to the town of Saumur, to Grandmère's tiny apartment and then to our hotel across from the Abbey with the graveyard alongside it where Papa would be buried. I slept for the entire ride, waking when Uncle Benjamin pulled the Citroën into the parking lot of Grandmère's building. I hadn't been there in a while, but nothing had changed. There were clusters of tall white buildings with bleakly colored shutters on each building. Grandmère lived in the building all the way to the left with the green shutters in an apartment on the first floor. She was crippled and too obese to get up stairs.

Papa told her on the phone that he had brain cancer, not AIDS. The word "SIDA" was not to be spoken once we got inside, Mai gently reminded me in the car.

Papa's oldest sister Yolaine opened the door and kissed each of our cheeks, twice. Her eyes were bloodshot from crying. Grandmère sat in the living room. All of Papa's siblings were there with her. Typically, they had nothing to do with her—she was excommunicated from their lives for her philandering when they were children and for her abandonment of them to take care of the children of another man: Papa's real father Henri. . . . As an old lady, she remained the villain, the home wrecker, but none of them were heartless enough not to visit her when she lost a child.

Grandmère usually oscillated between hysterical laughter and tears in short intervals of time, but it was only tears that day. Black layers of clothing covered her enormous, ailing body. All she could do was cry over the son that the townspeople once suspected was a bastard.

I was relieved when we left and headed to our hotel.

Sleep was never more inviting. I wanted to sleep and never wake up, but Mai woke me early the next morning to tell me that the burial was beginning shortly. In a daze, I walked past the abbey to the field where the graveyard was located.

I stopped at this stone that Papa showed me on each of our visits there together. It was the gravestone of a brother he never met who died from a rare lung infection before Papa was born—his name was Yannick.

Yannick was buried in a box as small as shoebox. He was so tiny. Just a few days old.

Papa's voice was speaking to me, telling me things, even as I noticed the funeral procession in the distance, and his coffin being carried toward the abyss dug into the dirt.

Sequestered off to the side, away from Papa's family, were a group of people whom I recognized: Henri . . . Papa's real father . . . his wife and two daughters.

Grandmère had informed Henri of Papa's death and asked him to attend the burial. She did not come. She stayed in her apartment.

I said nothing to Henri and barely spoke to anyone at all. All I could do was stare at the coffin.

As dirt was shoveled over his body, Papa's sister Claude started to scream. Her screaming was the rage inside me that I didn't know how to express. My family felt cursed, even though Uncle Benjamin promised at Papa's funeral ceremony in Florida that life still had good things in store for us all.

"Life never takes away without giving something back," he said and I tried to believe him.

Life would never be the same but it would go on. Luc would move cross country to California to live with Uncle Benjamin. I would graduate from Cornell the following year and head to New York City to try to become a writer.

Part Three
Bridges

CHAPTER THIRTY-THREE

THE ANONYMITY OF THE CITY was good for mourning. I loved that I could wander the streets alone for hours, observing the passersby, experiencing the full range of feelings that coursed through me: fear, rage, bleakness. . . . There was one to answer to, no one to please or impress with some more refined version of myself. It was just me with my own soul, amidst the city's frenetic energy, its lights, sound, and shadows.

Certain neighborhoods felt more like home than others. I quickly took to the feel of the East Village: the dimly lit hipster cafés that let you stay and write or read for hours, drinking variations of coffee drinks, exchanging smiles with strangers. The cheapish, chic restaurants where I'd get a table in the back or in a corner, alone with the company of my own thoughts . . . reveling in my solitude.

The time to be with myself was contagious. The more I had of it, the more I wanted and the richer the moments of insight became. I learned to tolerate the darkness with patience and willpower. When I let myself inhabit it, light flowed through. It was the surrender to my ghosts that stopped the haunting. To allow my feelings the right to be there, to welcome them without judgment, was to assist them in their journey toward departure. It was not an easy feat, but a prerequisite for the positive events in my life that followed.

So while each experience, interchange, and emotion that I had brought me back to the losses that marked my identity, I was growing resilient, more able to channel my pain in productive ways. I learned that the world was a welcoming recipient of the efforts I put forth.

CHAPTER THIRTY-FOUR

AT FIRST GLANCE, it would seem I found my therapist at random. A thick directory of health care providers was sitting on the desk of a job I was working at temporarily. Knowing that it would behoove me to start seeing someone on a frequent basis, I called one of the first providers I saw on the long list of psychiatrists. I learned upon meeting Dr. Yoo that she was also a specialist in psychoanalysis. She loved to analyze dreams and to consider the role that the unconscious played in emotions and behavior.

While I knew from the onset of my relationship with her that there was synergy between us, a deep respect that led to a healthy, therapeutic relationship, I didn't discover until years later that we had a remarkably similar past.

Dr. Yoo was orphaned young when her parents passed away in the Korean war. Her primary familial support became her uncle, a scholar who still lived in Korea. She respected him in a way that I respected Uncle Benjamin; he had become a mentor to her in the wake of her parents's deaths.

I couldn't help but feel from her disclosure, that it was more than coincidence that brought us together. It was the inexplicable and beautiful working of fate.

"I feel that for the most part I need to depend on myself," I said to her once.

"That is also my story," she replied.

And I know it is often the story of girls who lose mothers, specifically, in untimely ways. A girl's quest becomes defined by a need to depend on oneself, to nurture oneself, to dismiss the idea again and again that other people can fill one's voids.

While on a conscious level I searched to be mothered, the same narrative repeated itself. I could not replace my mother's unconditional love. But I could learn to love me. That was the control I was left with in spite of the loss. In the face of disappointment, I could always turn to myself and find comfort. My life had become about creating a safe space I could come to when people or life itself let me down. I became my own mother, which helped me survive.

CHAPTER THIRTY-FIVE

Since my freshman year of college, my immune system had been very weak. It worsened after Papa's death. Blood tests revealed nothing life threatening. All that showed was Chronic Epstein-Barr virus, also referred to in medical circles as "Chronic Mono." Yet, I was sick more than I was healthy. I regularly faced extreme exhaustion and muscle weakness, persistent nausea and incessant flus and colds. One bug would heal and another would come. I also had chronic headaches that seemed to defy any specific diagnosis, but resembled a cross between tension headaches and migraines.

In New York City, I was introduced through a friend to a mind/body healer/nutritionist whose approach to wellness inspired me to change many aspects of my lifestyle. The first vice to go was the overeating of junk food, which had been weakening my immune system. I eliminated alcohol and drugs. While I was never an addict, these substances still made me feel unhealthy and depressed. She advised me to speed walk on a daily basis, which cleared toxins out of my body and helped me to relax my mind. She also coached me on how I could stop my more severe headaches at their onset. When I felt a severe headache coming on, I could mentally stop it, prevent the onset and then the aftermath. I learned that we have more control than we think about what goes on in our bodies; if we will ourselves we can feel less pain.

The other modalities that I became drawn to were acupuncture and massage, in conjunction with Chinese herbal teas from an herbalist. On a down day with my health, acupuncture or massage treatment could turn the tides. I'd arrive sometimes at the Chinese healing center that I frequented, feeling completely desperate with frustration from not feeling well and leave feeling calm and invigorated.

My health has improved tremendously in recent years. My immune system is almost completely back to normal in the sense that I rarely have to call in sick to work. I admittedly still struggle with headaches but they are minor in severity in terms of what they were in the few years after Papa died.

CHAPTER THIRTY-SIX

WRITING, FURTHERMORE, was curative. I didn't write for fun or enjoyment, but to get through my downswings. It was my catharsis and sometimes I felt like a mere receptacle for the words that streamed through my mind, out through my pen, bringing me clarity about what my inner experience was.

I filled up notebooks so quickly, not knowing where the time went when I'd be focused on a thought and realize suddenly that *hours* had evaporated. I'd tried a series of jobs in the industries of publishing, advertising, and even sales, which were mismatches for my personality. Before deciding to go back to graduate school with the plan to become a teacher, I took six months to write. I mostly wrote fiction. Sometimes I wanted to write about losing my parents, but I still felt so perplexed by their untimely deaths that I wasn't sure what type of story I would tell.

CHAPTER THIRTY-EIGHT

Relative to the people I knew and the existence I came from in nouveau riche suburbia, my situation was an anomaly. One parent made sense. I knew several other people who had lost either a mother or a father in childhood, but none who'd lost two. My story always stunned people. It disquieted them. Sometimes in their expressions was this sense that there was more than met the eye, that I was holding something back. But I was being totally straightforward.

How did they die? Some people asked me outright while other people tiptoed around the question, indirectly eliciting an answer as their imaginations ran wild. *Was there an accident? Were they sick? Did they die together or separately?* The intrigue of it evoked the human tendency to want to see a horror movie that would give some sort of rise.

I was the sole member of my family who was forthright with people about what happened to Papa. Mai had told the truth to some of her and Papa's friends when Papa died in Florida, but my actual family was not forthcoming about the real information with their networks of people.

"He had AIDS." I said it again and again, routinely, each time I was asked. Being truthful vindicated it somehow. It challenged the stigma. I was representing his right not to feel shame though this was not the way he asked me to represent him. I appropriated his wish for secrecy with my own conviction that there should not be shame. A need for secrecy, in my book, implied shame. . . .

The real mystery to me was how my father got AIDS, as opposed to when. I knew that the blood brothers story he told me and Luc the night I flew down to Florida was a lie. He was too smart a man to share blood with an AIDS victim. The story about stopping at an accident on the Long Island Expressway and interfacing with AIDS-related blood was equally preposterous. And while it was more feasible that he caught it through a blood transfusion, I wasn't even sure that he'd ever *had* a transfusion. Nothing in my memory allowed me to recall him ever losing enough blood to require a transfusion. . . . Additionally, doctors that I spoke with informed me that blood was tested for HIV from fairly early on in the 1980s. So the likelihood of him receiving contaminated blood if he did have a transfusion was not really likely.

I suspected he contracted the virus through heroin. While he'd kept hard drugs away from me and Luc, we both knew that he was a heavy drinker. Furthermore, Papa's nephew from France who worked at his restaurants in both New York City and Florida told me he'd heard that when Mommy was sick, Papa was doing cocaine as well as having an affair with his coat-check lady. While these anecdotes (or rumors) about my father disturbed me immensely, I had to factor them in to how he could have acquired the virus. The leap that he would have done hard drugs other than cocaine seemed a more logical one than that he caught AIDS from a woman. Though I had no confirmation from anyone about his heroin usage, I figured it could have been a part of his life. After all, he'd been a chef in Manhattan in the 1980s. Drugs were rampant, specifically among people who had as much spare cash to throw around as he did. He might not have known what to do with his success. He'd been so poor as a child in France, and in America he was living the high life. His was your quintessential rags-to-riches tale, and I thought the success had gone to his head and he'd gone too far with his partying.

Mai said she knew nothing. (Papa told her the same exact stories that he told us.) Uncle Benjamin said he had no clue either about how Papa could have acquired the disease. Grandma and Grandpa didn't like to talk about it, let alone admit that Papa actually died from AIDS. They had the incredible capacity to bend truth to their will and create their own narratives.

Sometimes the "how" was replaced by "why" and the why did not ask for a logical, pragmatic answer but a spiritual one. Why was my family chosen for misfortune? Why did we differ from the families around us? Why was life so painful, and was there an overseer?

Just as a portal opened for my father when he was an adult that helped him to better understand his identity, ultimately, a portal was opened for me. While this didn't solve my spiritual questions and frustrations, it was a chance for a much deeper understanding of what my family endured. And while the truth that I learned sent me on an endless search, leaving a trail of unanswerable questions, what happened to my parents shone in vibrant light.

CHAPTER THIRTY-NINE

GIRLSALON STARTED in coffee shops in the East Village as a group of lesbian performers and artists. I'd printed promotional flyers and walked the streets below Fourteenth street to attract a downtown, creative crowd, taping the flyers on poster boards everywhere. Poster boards got quickly covered and my ad would get lost beneath the surface, but there was always a quick window of opportunity for my call to be seen.

Attention lesbian performers and artists . . .

Sometimes I waited at a café to welcome a large group of women, enthusiastic to speak about their projects and goals. Other times very few women showed up and the momentum was low. . . . I harbored doubts about an ongoing successful group, but on an upswing I had faith that my idea could grow into something meaningful.

The first salon that went further than just discussion and into the realm of performance took place in my Park Slope apartment. Women showed up with their poetry or stories to read, guitars to play, jokes to crack. I relished in the laughter and communal vibe, wanting a larger place than my 300-square-foot living room for people to gather. Girlsalon took place at different venues: The Rising Café in Park Slope and Bluestocking Women Bookstore, New York City's only women's bookstore that held artistic events regularly. I asked for an experimental slot on their calendar. The next step was to print 1,000 flyers, about 10 times more than my first print run. The show was open mic and there were a large number of interested participants who signed up. As the night passed, a crowd grew out the door, onto Allen Street where the venue was located.

I was then approached by Beth Greenfield, an editor at *Time Out* magazine, who made what I was trying to do known to her readership. Then came a huge stream of e-mails from people who read the article, wanting to add themselves to my growing list. Girlsalon was becoming a name through word of mouth, promoted through my website: janinesays.com.

It turned into a variety show and became a regular gig on the third Thursday night of each month at Meow Mix, the renowned hipster lesbian bar of the East Village. While aesthetically the venue was a run-down dive bar, it nurtured the spirit of women. The light of the talent that shown on the stage, varying from month to month, made the space a magnificent one that I cherished returning to.

While I'd set Girlsalon in motion, it had taken on a life of its own without me. There was a need out there for a forum for queer women. Recognizing how deep that need was created more impetus for me to continue putting forth efforts to make it successful.

My concept was that all women at all levels of ability should have a chance to get on stage. Thus, the event attracted women who had never held a microphone in their hand to women at the other end of the spectrum who were well-versed performers, trying to widen their reach.

Hosting Girlsalon inspired me to read my poetry. I self-published a chapbook called *Cathartic Ramblings*, which was sold at Bluestockings. Was this really me? On shelves? Getting invited to read at readings around town? Making my dreams come true? People laughed at my jokes that I told in between reading poems on stage. I think that I made a crowd feel comfortable because I was self effacing. And my ability to laugh at myself was much better than my self esteem. I really enjoyed stage time. A friend of mine commented once that when I was on stage it was as if I was sitting in my own living room!

Some nights were off nights. Perhaps I expected too much. An audience was not always reliably supportive. It depended on the mix of people, the chemistry in the room. Sometimes a crowd made me feel high, other times just totally small. Yet I knew it was my own feelings about myself that ultimately determined the mood that I went to sleep with at night. Self acceptance was much easier than self love . . . self love was an ongoing feat. It could fade as quickly as it came, so I had to be wary not to let it slip too far from my reach. . . .

The most incredible rewards from Girlsalon, by far, were the friendships I made, and the affinity I felt for the people I met. They were sisters with whom I shared important commonalities: a love of women, of art, ideas, and community space.

CHAPTER FORTY

THE KNOWLEDGE HAD GROWN within me that writing was healing. It was an honor to have the opportunity to share that with the kids of the YES (Youth Enrichment Services) program. I approached the directors of this program for LGBT youth (housed at The LGBT Center of New York City) when I started my certification in poetry therapy, a mode of art therapy that uses the written word as a modality for healing. They accepted me as a volunteer artist, and I began designing and running weekly workshops called *Writing Is Healing.*

I provided the attendees with poems or stories written by LGBT youth worldwide that introduced themes that they might be struggling with: confusion about identity, rejection from family, homophobia from society . . . then group members wrote on the theme of the week with a prompt I provided. The last part of session was a small salon where anyone had the option to share their work.

The group members were city youth of all ethnicities and social classes. Some were sure of being bisexual or gay while others were questioning. Some had homes to live in with family members who supported their alternative identities, while others were homeless, unclear where their next meals might be coming from. They'd been tossed to the streets just for being true to themselves about who they were.

I remember getting chills one day when a supervisor of mine asked me to throw away a slice of pizza that I was eating before my group started.

"Some of the kids around here don't get much to eat, so it's best not to eat around them," she said. I went into the bathroom to cry, realizing how blessed I'd been in my own life to have had money and food and a family and friends that loved me no matter what my sexual orientation was.

Some kids came to the group as ritual, week after week, month after month, while others came once with heartrending stories and then never showed up again. The story that most sticks out in my mind is that of a boy who looked no older than fifteen years old. He was pale and meek. He expressed to the group on his one-time drop-in that he'd slept with someone who was recently diagnosed with HIV and was scared to get a test. I was hoping he'd come back to group the following week, but he didn't. No one at The Center heard from him again.

I felt a passion toward working with kids even if it meant no more than giving than giving a reassuring smile, some words of advice, or a journal exercise that tapped into something inside them that needed release. I saw them cultivate their strengths through their writing. Simple writing prompts could open up worlds of confession, uncover wellsprings of previously untapped emotions. The positive feelings about volunteering led me to my future teaching career at colleges and high schools in the city.

And what had once felt shameful began to feel like a strength. It was helpful to encourage other people, specifically kids, to feel that it was okay to be who they were. As a teenage girl, my gay desire had made me feel so freakish and alone. To be a facilitator of their self acceptance and pride was an extraordinary experience for me.

February 2002
Five years after Papa's death

CHAPTER FORTY-ONE

THE PHONE RANG shortly after I arrived home from work. Uncle Benjamin was calling from Los Angeles. Sometimes he used this tone that unnerved me. "I need to tell you something very important," he said. It reminded me of a drunken, late-night confession.

"Okay," I said. "I'm listening."

"This is something that I probably should have told you a while ago, but every time I tried, I couldn't bring myself to do it. I didn't want to upset you more. But this information will give you perspective . . . so much more of your childhood will make sense to you. Puzzle pieces will start falling into place."

"Okay," I said.

"Your father first tested positive for HIV in 1986. You were only ten years old."

"*What? How do you know this?*"

"I was there," he said. "I was the first person he told. . . ."

In my mind's eye, I watched the scene unfold as Uncle Benjamin described it to me. It was 1986. Papa showed up at his Manhattan office. Late. A Tuesday afternoon. Shaken to the bone.

I need to talk to you man.

He was pale and frightened. He got an AIDS test from my mother's cousin, Jessica Schwartz, who was a doctor, and the test came back positive. He said he had no clue why. One thing he speculated on was a blood transfusion he got at the hospital after cutting himself at work with a butcher knife. He also said that he stopped once at an accident on the Long Island Expressway on the way home from work, and he helped pull people out of the car at the accident site. Blood spilled onto him. He could have had an open cut, since he frequently had open cuts from mishaps in the kitchen.

Uncle Benjamin continued to narrate the most fateful day in my family's history. The day inevitably where everything changed and where any normality was crushed. Any semblance of peace and joy that followed was illusion. AIDS in 1986 was a death sentence. There was just no way to come out from under its pitch black cloud—one could just pretend to be standing in the sunshine.

A meeting was summoned in the library of my old house in Roslyn. The room of secrets. Eavesdrop with drinking glasses, but walls were thick. You would only catch snippets of truth. You would not put the whole story together. You weren't meant to. You were just a child. Children were to be seen and not heard. And secrets were to be kept from children. Lies were to be told. To protect them. Nightlights were to be kept on.

Luc and I were sent to the playroom to watch television. Perhaps we watched *Family Ties, The Facts of Life, Growing Pains,* or *Webster.* . . . But no upper middle-class suburban family on a television sitcom would go through what we went through. None would be ravaged by AIDS. The sounds of 1986 television kept us distracted from my mother learning, just upstairs, that her perfect, pretty, affluent, suburban life was through and through.

She was screaming hysterically, beside herself with grief. Grandma and Grandpa had no time at all to process their own fear. They needed to calm their child down. They were her protectors. In the moment, my mother did not trust my father— she was furious at him. She didn't believe any of his excuses.

This was not the case of a histrionic person. This was a woman learning that her husband would die; his hourglass was flipped, the sand was slipping down. She just needed to turn on the news, prime time to confirm it. This was a woman who had to have thought that she was sick. After all, she was his wife.

"How did you get this?" she demanded. She had the very same question for Papa in 1986 that Luc and I had on his deathbed in Florida in 1997.

How did you get this Papa?

Papa was ambiguous. Different stories emerged, each which implied his innocence: a harmless blood brothers pact with a boyhood friend, a martyr at an accident scene on the Long Island Expressway, the victim of a swift butcher knife in the kitchen at work.

Uncle Benjamin told me that there was a history of cheating in my parents's marriage. He said that my mother first learned about Papa's affairs with other women when she found condoms in the glove compartment of his car, years before. She made him move out, but then they reconciled and had that second wedding in 1984. Two years before the HIV diagnosis even happened . . .

"Why did she take him back?" I asked.

"Because that is what your grandparents pushed her to do. And she listened to what they said. She idolized them . . . particularly Grandpa. His opinion was that when you marry someone it's for better or worse. She chose him to marry, so she had to live with him."

Mommy finally calmed down and stopped screaming. Grandpa was able to speak some sense to her. He managed to get her focused on a priority that would take precedence over everything, a priority that would distract her from her own panic.

"This must be kept secret. No one outside the family can ever know," Grandpa preached.

He hammered the fear of god into both of my parents. He said that if anyone learned about the AIDS, Papa would lose his business. No one would want a chef with AIDS. People would spread rumors and blackball the restaurant. Papa would lose his livelihood. He'd be unable to make mortgage payments. We'd have to sell our house. Papa was not an educated man—he was but an immigrant without a college degree. He was a chef and only that. If he couldn't cook, what would he do? How would he support us?

Grandpa's fear was contagious. My parents heeded his call. Absolutely *no one* could know. Not friends . . . not even best friends. *No one.* Uncle Benjamin and Aunt Karen were sworn to secrecy. No one outside of the library, that cozy sanctuary of secrets, including the two small children downstairs naively watching television could know a thing.

The motivation for keeping things secret from me and Luc, Uncle Benjamin explained to me, was that the information would scare the hell out of us. We would walk through our childhoods with constant trepidation. Everything innocent and beautiful and special would instantly be stolen from us. We would be children who never felt a moment's peace.

The other factor was that we could not be trusted with that kind of serious information. One of us, or both of us, not realizing the gravity of the situation, would slip the information to a friend at school who would slip to his parents who would slip to their friends. Gossip, which spreads in a nouveau riche Long Island town like the bubonic plague, would turn my parents and their children into the Roslyn lepers. Parents wouldn't want their children to be around us.

We would be ostracized at school, called the AIDS kids. Teased. Tortured. Perhaps even killed.

"Hate crimes are out there," Grandpa admonished.

For years, Uncle Benjamin kept my parents's secret, only discussing it with the immediate family. When Papa got fatally sick, Uncle Benjamin pretended to have just found out. So did Grandma and Grandpa. I was too absorbed in my own grief to realize that they just were not shocked . . . for eleven years, they knew that Papa's untimely death would come. Unless there was a cure . . .

I asked Uncle Benjamin whether Mommy was HIV positive and whether Mai knew the truth about Papa's HIV status all along. To both questions, Uncle Benjamin had precisely the same answer.

"I don't know."

He said he'd asked my mother several times about her HIV status, expressing the significance to her of being tested for the disease.

"She said she didn't want to know, that she couldn't live with the knowing. She would shut me up if I even breached the topic and say that it was none of my business. Your mom was a very private person. As for Mai, I assumed that your father told her the truth. I asked him at some point after they started dating if he was being safe and he said, "Yeah man, of course."

"But you never asked him if he actually told her?"

"No. I didn't feel it was my place."

CHAPTER FORTY-TWO

I STARTED WALKING aimlessly through a cold Brooklyn night. Uncle Benjamin was calling Luc to tell him what he had told me. In a similar instant, he would have his childhood re-framed and he would do what he would with it. We were very different people. While I would become an impassioned investigator, Luc would try not to dwell too much on the past.

I hadn't made it far from home when the epiphany hit me: it was not a question of whether Mommy was *also* HIV positive, but that her "cancer" was AIDS. It was always AIDS. It was so obvious once I lined up the facts, aware of the chronology. Papa gave her HIV; her cancer was just the opportunistic infection that killed her. She would be alive were it not for him. He *killed* her. The father that I'd thought of as wild and reckless had taken on a new role in my mind: murderer. I hated him then for taking my only mother from me, for my eleven years bereft of a mother's love. I knew that he wouldn't have infected her intentionally, but that didn't change the fact that he was at fault, that he played a crucial role in her death.

It was impossible for me to believe that my family mem-bers hadn't pieced this together if they had really known the timeline. My assumption, initially, was that Uncle Benjamin wasn't telling me the full story which was not improbable considering that I'd just found out that my whole life had been packed with lies. He had to still be concealing something. He'd known the chronology of events for sixteen years. It was 2002. Papa was diagnosed in '86. (And could have contracted it a few years earlier.) Mommy got "cancer" in '88. She died in '91. How could he not have deduced that this was precisely what happened? She was a married woman exposed to HIV who died from a sarcoma. I remembered the word sarcoma; it had always stayed etched in my inventory of words.

I called him from my cell phone. My fingers were numb and my hands were shaking as I walked. I knew that what happened to her was not the work of a childhood ski accident that somehow created a tumor that turned cancerous. That narrative was fabricated, and it was maintained by the whole family's denial of the truth.

My theory was "possible" Uncle Benjamin said, while it was not something he ever conceived of before, he added, vouching that it was the same for Aunt Karen, Grandma and Grandpa. He even said that to his knowledge my parents did not make that connection.

"But how can that be?"

"We all just thought the cancer she came down with was completely unrelated."

"How could you have?"

"She always had a problem with her right foot. Since before you were even born. When a tumor was found there it made sense why she always had that pain. I don't think we were thinking about HIV playing a role."

"But don't you find it uncanny that she never had a malignant tumor until two years after Papa was diagnosed with HIV?"

"I never thought about it that way," Uncle Benjamin said. "I don't think any of us did. I'm being honest with you."

Was I really from this family? How could I be the only one this occurred to? What made me different? Even Luc was hesitant to believe what I was telling him when I called him to tell him what I figured out. I felt like some sort of conspiracy theorist, but knew that I was simply crashing into blockades of denial. My mother's death from AIDS was difficult for everyone to admit to because of the sad implications.

Aunt Rachel, Uncle Benjamin's second wife, wanted to speak to me. She said that she saw my point perfectly. Not only did she see my point, but she said it was also her conviction that my mother died of AIDS. She had studied AIDS intensively in graduate school and knew about its progression.

"Your mom obviously had a problem with her foot for much of her life—it could have been anything—a pinched nerve, a cyst, maybe even a benign tumor that probably never would have metastasized into cancer."

"She screamed about that foot since I was a little kid," I said. "It could not have been a malignant tumor from the time I was four. She'd have been dead years before. I doubt cancer was in the picture then."

"I agree," Aunt Rachel said. "It's when HIV got into her

system that it attacked an area of weakness in her body and the malignancy developed."

I didn't need what a lawyer needed—proof beyond the shadow of a doubt. It was my mother's life and death I was considering, and I was convinced that she would be alive were it not for my father.

I think I was relieved that I finally had someone to blame. . . .

CHAPTER FORTY-THREE

IN MY MOST IMMEDIATE SEARCHING, I sat with my lap top trying to find answers about a connection between my mother's cancer and AIDS. I dove headfirst into the mammoth sea of Google.com, searching for any information that linked AIDS to Synovial Sarcoma. (After a short and unexplained phone call to my grandparents I'd learned that my mother's cancer was called Synovial Sarcoma.) No entries discussed the explicit possibility of a link between the two. Yet in my study of the broader area of "soft tissue cell cancers" of which Synovial Sarcoma was categorized, I read that HIV infection was a risk factor. I also read that the cause of Synovial Sarcoma was not always known.

I then spoke with a hotline at the National Cancer Institute. I was told that their literature did not explicitly list HIV as a cause for Synovial Sarcoma, but that knowledge about AIDS-related cancers was still murky territory.

Synovial Sarcoma is actually an extremely rare cancer, found predominantly in children. It accounts for few of the documented cases of cancer each year in the United States. Uncle Benjamin told me that the doctors were very surprised at the time that Mommy even had this type of cancer. What they weren't factoring in was HIV as a precipitating factor. This type of cancer itself was extremely rare and being AIDS-related was probably even rarer, which leads to little available information on the topic even now. The cancers most named as having connection to AIDS are Kaposi's sarcoma and varied forms of melanoma.

CHAPTER FORTY-FOUR

A BITCHY SECRETARY answered the phone, the gatekeeper for the oncologists who treated Mommy. Their practice was still flourishing in Port Washington, Long Island.

"Hold please," she said. Her voice exuded nastiness, impatience, the stress of answering phones.

"Can I help you?" she finally demanded.

"I am calling to see if can have a conversation either Doctor Thomas or Martino regarding my mother who was a patient of theirs."

"What is this regarding?"

"It's regarding some questions I have about my mom, who died eleven years ago. I want to see if I can get access to her medical records."

"Well, I can tell you right off the bat that the answer is no. We don't keep patient records after seven years."

"Where do they go?"

"They get shredded."

"Shredded?"

"Yes. Shredded. They get thrown out."

"Oncology records get thrown out? What about relatives that might need the information?"

"That's our policy here."

"Well, regardless," I said. *There was a plane crash in the ocean with my mother's body missing, never to wash up at shore.* "I'd like to speak with the doctors. Maybe they remember my mom."

"I doubt it," she said. "If it was over ten years ago."

"How do *you* know what either of them remembers? If you don't get me through to one of them NOW, I'm going to subpoena the medical records and talk to them about your attitude problem."

"Hold, please," she said, hitting the mute button. When she returned, she said, "Look, it's been a hectic morning around here. Why don't I take your name and number, and one of the doctors will get back to you at his earliest convenience."

Doctor Thomas called me later that afternoon.

"Thank you for getting back to me so quickly," I said. "I appreciate it."

"No problem. What can I do for you?"

"My mother was a patient of yours. She died in 1991."

"Yes. I remember Ilene. She was a very sweet woman."

"Well, I learned very recently that my father tested positive for HIV in 1986, two years before my mother got sick. Did you know anything about that?"

"No . . . I can't say that I did."

"My mom never expressed any fear about exposure?"

"No, never. And we wouldn't have tested for HIV then either. It was really not protocol at that time to even *ask* our cancer patients for an AIDS test. Nonetheless, even now, patients have the right of refusal. In New York State law, a patient can refuse a test. We can suggest it, but ultimately it's up to the patient."

"But you didn't suggest one to my mother?"

"No. Not that I recall."

"Would you have even considered that a married, heterosexual woman from Long Island was HIV positive?"

"I didn't personally suspect it about your mom, no."

"As an oncologist, would you say that it is possible that my mother's cancer was connected to AIDS?"

"I would say that it is possible, yes. It might not have been what happened, but in my professional opinion I'd say that, yes, it is possible."

CHAPTER FORTY-FIVE

ON THE EVENING of Uncle Benjamin's startling phone call he'd mentioned that the person who tested Papa for HIV was Mommy's first cousin, a dermatologist named Jessica Schwartz. Jessica was never married and never had any children. She was the daughter of Simon Schwartz, who lent Papa the money to open up *La Vie*, Grandma's sister Sylvia's daughter.

"Why would *she* of all people have tested him?" I'd asked.

"I don't know . . . it was very peculiar. Maybe your dad suspected that he was sick and he wanted a family member to confide in."

"It wasn't like they were close."

"Maybe they were. I know she used to go eat at the restaurant a lot when she lived in New York City."

"Well, I'm going to call her."

Jessica lived in Hawaii where she'd taken up residence since her retirement from medicine.

"My Uncle Benjamin told me that you gave my father an AIDS test in 1986," I said.

"Yes, that's correct," Jessica said.

"Why were you testing my father for HIV in the first place?" I asked.

"I wouldn't have gone to bed with any man without testing him first," Jessica conceded after a long pause. "Not in the midst of an AIDS scare in the country. I was too smart for that. I was a physician. I had my wits about me—especially then."

"So you were planning to sleep with my father? When you were my mother's cousin?"

"He came on to me," she said. "And I wasn't *necessarily* going to sleep with him."

"Then why did you need to give him an AIDS test, Jessica?"

"Just in case."

"So what happened when it came back positive?"

"Well, I called him and asked him to come over to my apartment. I lived on the Upper East Side then. I remember that sad day very clearly," she said, pensively. "He couldn't believe it. I kept telling him it was true, and he kept saying he didn't believe it until finally he broke down sobbing. We cried together for quite a while on the stoop of my building and then he went home."

"Did you ever speak to my mother about this after you diagnosed him?"

"No. Never. Your dad said that he would inform his family—which, in all fairness, he did."

"But Jessica, you were a *doctor* and my mom was your *cousin*. Didn't you think that you should have gone to her and spoken to her about it and urged her to get herself tested? She was your *family*. And it was AIDS."

"It was not really within my rights to do that. There were rules to follow. I had to protect your father's confidentiality.

I really could not discuss anything with her even if I wanted to."

"But when my mom was sick you came to see her several times. I remember you visiting her at my house in Roslyn. You never made a connection between the cancer she came down with and my father's HIV?"

"I didn't say anything to your mom or dad or your grandparents, but I'm going to be very frank with you and tell you that I was extremely suspicious that the sarcoma she had was AIDS-induced. Highly suspicious."

"Okay. Well, all this really pisses me off."

"Your father was a wonderful man," Jessica said. "Don't be angry at him about hitting on me. It was the Eighties. Everyone was sleeping with everyone. Don't hold any grudges against him."

"Okay, Jessica. Thanks for your advice and thanks for your time." *And go fuck yourself.*

Perhaps radiation and chemotherapy were not the best treatments for an AIDS patient with an already compromised immune system. I remembered the way that chemotherapy destroyed my mother: the paleness, the gauntness, the nausea . . . could chemo have saved her or was she treated in vain? Perhaps if Jessica had encouraged her to get tested she could have avoided that sort violence to her body. If she'd heard about the importance of getting tested from a doctor in her family, perhaps she'd have listened.

It bothered me tremendously that her own doctors didn't have the crucial piece about her exposure to AIDS.

She slipped by them without suspicion, protecting her secret, Grandpa's ominous words in her head never to tell a soul. It was difficult for me to believe that he meant even the doctors in charge of her health. Those paid hundreds of thousands of dollars to look after her wellness and to serve her their best were without a clue about what was really going on. The fear that the word could get out was stronger than the fear that she could undergo more suffering.

I imagined what Mommy went through again and again, day after day. I dreamed of her for months. And I dreamed that I *was* her. In my dreams, Papa was my lover and I just found out he had HIV, and I was terrified. I woke up again and again sweating, my heart palpitating. What was it like to withhold from her doctors what was a crucial part of her medical situation? What was it like to withhold from every close friend what was really going on for her, not expressing the hell she was living in, having virtually no outlets for sharing? Every last phone call I made to the network of friends Mommy had in her life (her very best friends included: Ronnie, Ronda, Joanie, and Terry) confirmed to me that no one knew what was going on. No one knew she had problems in her marriage, no one knew that Papa had HIV, or that Mommy was at dire risk. She was festering in her secret alone, with Papa as her only confidant.

The position she was in was nearly unthinkable, yet I couldn't stop thinking about it, couldn't stop wondering precisely what she thought and felt. I contemplated the moments she kept to herself and never shared, even with Papa, her ally and her nemesis at the same time. I tried to enter the silence in the spaces behind the words where she lived all the way from the disclosure of Papa's diagnosis in 1986 to her death in April of 1991. I was so very curious to know what she'd really believed, what stories she told herself to push onward in her everyday life while raising her two children. I wished that I could speak to her to ask her these questions, the questions that would reveal so much more of her identity. The desire to understand her, to compare her and juxtapose her to myself was a new kind of quest in my life.

CHAPTER FORTY-SIX

MY PLANE LANDED IN FLORIDA. A cool breeze with no chill wafted against me as I hailed a cab. As my taxi left the airport in Fort Lauderdale, speeding up to Interstate 95 North, I called Grandma and Grandpa to let them know that I was on my way. They had no idea that my visit was more than to drop in on them in their old age, to pay them company. My goal was to get answers that only they had.

They awaited me on a bench outside of their condominium when my taxi arrived. Grandpa was smoking a cigarette, cane in hand. His two strokes, the first of which was in 1987, mysteriously just one year after Papa's HIV diagnosis, had compromised his walking abilities, but his mind was still sharp. Grandma, dressed in a white-flowered sweat suit, rose to greet me as I glanced at the screen that reflected the price from the airport. She opened her purse.

"Twenty-five dollars. That seems like an awful lot," she noted, shaking her head.

"That's what it is Grandma," I laughed. "He drove me straight here. No diversions at all."

"Okay," she nodded. Sometimes she acted like she was still living in the 1930s and that prices should reflect that era.

When we arrived upstairs, I relaxed into the routine of Grandma giving me fresh towels and setting up the pull-out cot in the living room. Grandpa nearly instantly turned on CNN. Both of my grandparents loved to know what was going on in the world. They harped on the truth of what was "out there." But when it came to their own lives, they made up stories. They've told themselves so many stories that they may have forgotten what is actually real.

When they went to sleep, I lay on a lounge chair on the screened in patio and watched the stars and the ripples of aquamarine water shining off the lighted swimming pool, which was chiseled into the lawn of their retirement community. This was the first time I was visiting since Uncle Benjamin's phone call. There was no way to push away the tinge of all that my grandparents endured that they never spoke to me about. Melancholy filled me. Pictures of Papa hung throughout the apartment. One that was framed, in the living room, featured him with his arms around Grandpa and Uncle Benjamin. Another taped onto the refrigerator showed him holding Luc and me at sleepaway camp when we were children. A larger frame on a dining room shelf showed him and Mommy at their wedding. Which stories were they telling themselves about my father . . . responsible for their daughter's death? Which narratives allowed them to live out their elderly years most peacefully?

We ate dinner the following night at a seafood restaurant near the coast. Grandma and Grandpa shared the same dish they shared each time: the coconut shrimp.

"Uncle Benjamin told me that Papa knew that he had HIV since 1986," I said.

"When did he tell you that?" Grandpa asked me after a prolonged pause.

"Recently. A few months ago."

"Why did he do that?" Grandma threw her hands up, turning to Grandpa in exasperation. "What was the point of that?" she demanded from my grandfather who stayed quiet.

"Because he wanted me and Luc to know the truth Grandma," I answered.

"I'm not sure it was '86," Grandma stumbled. "I can't even remember the time line anymore."

"And I'm not convinced," Grandpa stepped in, "That it was ever really HIV at all."

"Grandpa . . . that's ridiculous. Papa died of AIDS in 1997. You know that. Come on."

"No. I'm not totally convinced. Mistakes are made all of the time. That's what I learned after years of working in the insurance business. Mistakes happen. When your father got diagnosed years ago, he had a duplicate test done in Paris and it came back negative. So I am still not convinced that it was AIDS."

"Are you trying to tell me that in March of 1997, my father did not *definitively* die from AIDS?"

"I'm not saying one thing or another; all I'm saying is that I'm not convinced of it because mistakes are made."

"When Papa told you that he was HIV positive in 1986, did you tell Mommy that she had to get an AIDS test?"

"She was fine," Grandma said, emphatically.

"But did you tell her that she should take an AIDS test?"

"Well, that would have made sense, of course," Grandma nodded pausing. "Yes. She was tested. And she was fine."

"*When* was she tested Grandma? *Where* was she tested?"

"I can't remember exactly."

"You know," Grandpa interjected. "When your mother got sick with that cancer, they did tons of blood work. If anything was wrong it would have come out in the open. I can't begin to tell you how many doctors took her blood. There was no AIDS. Believe me. Get that idea out of your mind. There was no AIDS."

"Okay Grandpa, but Grandma is saying that Mommy was tested *before* she got sick. Right?"

"That's woman stuff," Grandpa said finally. "Grandma would know better." I turned back to my grandmother.

"Grandma, was she tested? *Before* she got sick with cancer?"

"It would have made sense. Of course." Grandma said, excusing herself then from the table to go to the bathroom.

"I really don't want to talk about this anymore," she said. "It upsets me."

"When your mom got sick with cancer," Grandpa continued with Grandma gone, "we didn't want to put more pressure on her. We didn't want to make her worry about an AIDS test. She had a lot on her mind, too much to worry about. She started all the treatments then for cancer and believe me, if there was anything *at all* wrong with her blood the doctors would have picked up on it! We would have known. Believe me."

I nodded my head, pretending to be in synch with his tale. I could see that he held true to his belief with the fervor of religious faith and what he was telling me was what he needed to believe.

"I have another question Grandma," I said her when she returned to the table. "Do you know *when* Papa told Mai that he had HIV?"

"When your Papa got sick . . . she found out," Grandma said.

"When he got sick in 1997?"

"Right. Of course she found out then . . . he was sick . . . he had to tell her what was wrong."

"But Grandma, Papa knew for *eleven years* that he had HIV. Did he tell her sooner than 1997?"

"I don't know. I just know that he told her when he got sick, then, in Florida."

"So when he was dating her, did you ever suspect that he could be keeping this information from her?"

"It wasn't something we thought about," Grandpa stepped back in. "It was none of our business."

"So when Mai seemed totally shocked in 1997 that Papa had AIDS, what did you guys think? What was your reaction?"

"Please don't say bad things about your father," Grandma said, her voice shaky. "Please. Let's stop this conversation. I want to stop this conversation. This conversation is upsetting me." I looked at Grandpa who nodded.

On the car ride on the way home from the ocean, Grandma reminded me that Papa was a good man, that he always provided for Mommy and for his children. He'd made some indiscretions by cheating on Mommy with other women, but he redeemed himself when he took care of her when she was sick.

"Don't ever think badly of your father," she said to me. "Please don't think badly of your father."

CHAPTER FORTY-SEVEN

WHAT MAI HAD KNOWN or hadn't known about Papa's HIV status was an enigma. I couldn't decide whether she had been a victim of his secrecy or whether she had misrepresented what she had known for the sake of protecting his wishes.

If there had been any miracle thus far, it was that Mai was healthy: in the clear . . . HIV negative. She said that her doctors referred to her as a "miracle" case; they claimed she possessed what was referred to in medical circles as a miracle gene. She had a genetic immunity to the HIV virus that was rare in the human species. While she had been repeatedly exposed to the HIV virus through unprotected sex with my father, she remained negative. Her blood had been analyzed in Washington, D.C., and it was determined that she could not contract the AIDS virus, no matter what. Something in her blood rejected HIV.

Uncle Benjamin and Luc and I would try to figure out the truth, unable to settle with one answer. One possibility seemed to quickly deconstruct another. It was a riddle impossible to solve. There were different scenarios I played out in my mind, trying to get to the truth.

The first went as such: Papa went to Club Med in Martinique in January of 1992, nine months after my mother's death. He met Mai on the airplane. They became lovers. Before they were ever intimate, Papa told her he was HIV positive and she said that while it upset her, she was attracted to him and that they would just practice very safe sex. She didn't get HIV because they were safe, the miracle gene story was a lie, and she'd only told me they'd had unprotected so not to make me suspicious that she'd known all along. Her motive for concealing it from me and Luc was because Papa didn't want us to know that he'd known about his sickness all of those years. Not only would it have made him appear dishonest in our eyes, but it also could have sparked the idea in our minds that he'd made Mommy sick.

Second possibility: Papa went to Club Med in Martinique in January of 1992, nine months after my mother's death. He met Mai on the airplane. They became lovers. He thought that if he told her right away that he was HIV positive that she would be uninterested in seeing him further. Instead, he rationalized to himself that he would be very safe by always using condoms. When they decided to be in a monogamous, committed relationship he decided to tell her the truth. She was totally furious at his confession, but she had already fallen in love with him and saw a path to forgiveness.

Another: Papa went to Club Med in Martinique in January of 1992, nine months after my mother's death. He met Mai on the airplane. They became lovers. He thought that if he told her the truth that she would not want to pursue him any further. So he kept his secret from her . . . even after they professed love to one another and decided to be in an exclusive relationship. After using condoms for quite a while, Mai told him that condoms were not really necessary: she'd had her tubes tied after her divorce from her first husband, Pedro, the father of her two children. Papa was in a bind. If she did not want to use condoms anymore, he had to tell her the truth if he wanted to ensure that she was safe. He told her he was positive and her reaction was rage. She felt deceived and struggled with herself about whether to stay or go. As angry as she was, she was deeply in love with him and also did not want to be alone after devoting so much time to him already. She eventually found it in herself to forgive him. They continued to use condoms, which is why she stayed HIV negative.

Then there was a much darker scenario. In this scenario, Papa was not just responsible for my mother's death, but had knowingly deceived Mai. A narcissist who saw his own need for love and security more invaluable than someone else's life. He met her in January of 1992. He was a widower for nine months, lonely and scared. He was wary of dating someone exclusively because he knew that he had HIV. On their first few encounters, he didn't know if she was just ephemeral, a ship passing in the night. He was irresponsible and selfish in that he didn't tell her he was HIV positive, yet he used adequate protection, rationalizing to himself that she'd be safe. Yet time pressed on and she was still in his life, not going away. A deep affinity had grown between them. They shared strangely similar stories of their pasts. Neither had known their real fathers growing up. Neither of their real fathers had taken any interest in them, despite knowing that they existed. And they shared the love of the French language and traveling. Mai became his companion to see the world that he wanted to see before he died. She was an excellent traveling cohort and accompanied him to Brazil, Europe, and Asia. She showed him Vietnam, her roots, where he came down with a disturbing case of shingles, not sharing with her that it could be HIV-induced.

She became more and more indispensable to him, and the more he wanted her in his life, the harder it was to tell her the truth because it would not just mean his potential abandonment, but also a massive shift in perception of him. His outward display of confidence was balanced by a sadly frail core. Deep down, he did not really believe that he was worthy. A child whose mother abandons him never truly believes in his own value, even when that child grows up. He knew that if he told her his secret, he would most likely be abandoned again and left alone with HIV. He'd be closer to his death than he'd been when he met her, and he'd die alone without being loved, except by his children.

He rationalized that he would protect her, be safe, always use condoms. But as they stayed monogamous, she started to ask questions. Her tubes were tied after her divorce from her first husband, Pedro. He couldn't explain to her why in the context of their long term relationship he had to use condoms. The deeper he got into his own lie, the harder it was for him to extricate himself. And after so many years of being healthy, running marathons around the cities of the world, and staying healthy with no visible signs of sickness, he even thought that perhaps he had beat AIDS. Grandpa Levy told him that maybe he could beat it. Yet he always knew somewhere inside of him that he was putting her at risk. But Mai really was among the rare percentage of humans who did not contract the HIV virus upon exposure. She had the uncanny luck that most people wouldn't have had.

He was on trial in my mind. Was her tale about her miracle gene all just one great big Academy Award–winning act, a production that only an ingenious actress could pull off or had my father engaged in criminal behavior for concealing information that could have killed her or otherwise made her chronically sick? One voice spoke as his prosecutor, and another spoke as his defense attorney. I just couldn't bring myself to call the most important witness to the stand—I was afraid of hurting her, of bringing her more pain if Papa had really betrayed her. Unfortunately, I suspected that he did. The prosecution had a much more compelling argument than the defense.

I had a guilty conscience for two years. In conversing with her each time I did, I kept what I knew to myself, feeling immobilized each time I tried to tell her. But I knew that no one in my family was planning to level with her. If she didn't know the truth already, she wasn't going to find it out from anyone but me.

For the two years that I kept on a nightlight for Mai, I was plagued by guilt.

Mai had struggled continually since Papa's death. He was the second man she'd committed to in her life and even with the possibility that she had known he would get sick, nothing could have matched the fact the he did and that she sacrificed her needs to cater to his. I'm not completely sure why she moved back to France after he died. Perhaps it was because he was buried there and she wanted to be closer to him. She settled in the French Riviera, a few hours from where he was buried in Font D'Vreau. After living there for a little while, she became involved with another man, Jean-Claude, who was jealous of my father's memory, and didn't want her to have contact with his children. Finally, growing tired and fed up with his controlling ways, she moved with very little money to Scottsdale, Arizona, where she practiced massage therapy and got involved with *Course in Miracles*. She faced a long depression although faith in a higher power helped her prevail. She then went back to France again where she fell in love with another man, Philippe, who was also a chef. They planned to move to the States together to live back in Florida, just across the coast from where she had lived with Papa in Naples. She finally seemed happy again. I knew her grief would never go away, but she was doing well in her life in light of the trauma she'd been through.

If she'd been deceived by Papa, which I suspected she had been, my phone call would throw off her world again, as Uncle Benjamin's phone call had thrown off mine. But it would be for the best. She deserved the truth it if was available. It was hers to have.

"Mai," I said. "There's something that I need to talk to you about."

"Okay."

"Are you telling me the truth when you tell me that you had no idea that my father had HIV before he got sick in 1997?"

"Yes. Of course. I am telling you the truth."

"Well, what I found out, about three years ago, was that my father knew that he was HIV positive since 1986. I was ten years old when he first got diagnosed."

On the line was a prolonged silence followed by heaving sobs. I knew they were authentic.

"He *knew*? How did you find this out?"

"My Uncle Benjamin told me. My father told him, my mother, and my grandparents when he found out in 1986. I'm convinced that mother's cancer was AIDS-related. She contracted it from him. Her sarcoma was AIDS-induced. There's no conclusive proof of it, but I'm sure that it's what happened. My father tested positive in '86 and my mother got sick in 1988. She got treated for cancer without even being tested for AIDS. Her doctors didn't suspect anything and she didn't tell them she'd been exposed.

"Your poor mom," she said. "I can only imagine what she went through. I had my suspicions she could have contracted it from him, but I never wanted to say anything to you because I didn't want to upset you unnecessarily."

"Somehow you were spared though," I said. "Through this genetic immunity to AIDS. That's true, right?"

"Yes. My blood is in Washington, D.C. It's being looked at in the search for a vaccine for AIDS."

"That's amazing."

"What luck," she said.

"I know that this is hard to hear Mai."

"I am very glad you shared this with me," she said. "It is better for me to know the truth."

Sometimes I go back to envision the crushing feeling of realizing that someone who you loved and nursed through sickness and death betrayed you. I also imagine what it was like to have had the unfathomable luck that she had: to have beat a disease like AIDS despite repeated exposure.

I was far more furious at my father than she was though it was her life that was put at risk.

Children: Please do not harbor any anger toward your father on behalf of me. While what he did to me was wrong and selfish, I do not believe it was in any way malicious. Reflecting upon it now, in retrospect, so many things are clearer to me. I do feel now that there was something that he wanted to tell me, but couldn't muster the courage to do so. He was a coward, but not evil. And he was punished enough through the way he died for the mistakes he made in his life. It will only hurt YOU to be angry; it will not help you in your healing. Please forgive him. I hope you take my words to heart.

Love, Mai

But the sadness that I carried around in the past had morphed into a righteous anger. It played out sometimes in unforeseen moments with just about anyone who pushed my buttons, whose mannerisms or style irritated me. There was this seething I experienced when provoked. Sometimes I spent the whole day fuming mad.

I questioned why Papa was the person he'd been and wondered if I possessed the similar ability to do something so wrong. I couldn't understand why he'd done something so reckless, how he could have watched Mommy die in front of him and then had the audacity to leave another woman unprotected from AIDS. Didn't he know, didn't he realize that he had *killed* her? And even if he did not, it infuriated me that he could have done what he did to Mai, no matter what the excuse was. Even if he had never consciously thought he had killed my mother, what gave him the right to expose another woman to this deathly virus? It was unconscionable, and I judged him more harshly than anyone else, although Luc thought that what he did was equally reprehensible.

Ironically, as his children, we were the angriest about how he'd treated Mai. Perhaps it was because we were an extension of him and felt somehow responsible for who he'd been, even if we'd had absolutely no bearing on the decisions that he made when he was alive. What allowed Luc to forgive him more quickly for his transgression was Luc's memory of how he died.

"You weren't there," he said to me. "You just didn't see how he already paid the price. He became pathetic."

I tried to forgive him with Luc's words, but the rage continued on. There was an estrangement I felt toward him that had not been there before knowing about this betrayal. I thought that I stopped loving him. He was no longer worthy of my love or my respect. He'd crossed boundaries that were indefensible, and had made irrevocable mistakes.

CHAPTER FORTY-EIGHT

HELENA AND MICHAEL LIBRETT were old friends of my parents. I hadn't seen much of them since I was younger, but they always made an effort to keep in touch with me, specifically after Papa died. I saw them only occasionally since his death in 1997; one of the few times was when they invited me to their adopted son Logan's birthday party in 2004, over two years after Uncle Benjamin's crazy phone call.

What's strange is that I wouldn't have gone to the birthday party if my girlfriend at the time had not been going upstate that day to visit her family. I didn't have a car, but was glad to hear that we could take the train together. Michael called me very last minute to tell me about the impromptu gathering for Logan. Plans fell into place hastily.

At the party, a man approached me who I didn't recognize. He introduced himself as Alain.

"I haven't seen you since you were a little girl," Alain said, "I used to come to your parents's pool parties in Roslyn. Then I bought a business in Florida, and I saw your dad from time to time down there before he died."

Alain introduced me to his wife, Michelle. We made small talk for a while when Michelle said, "I didn't think that Mai was very good for your father. I always thought your mother was a much better match for him."

While for years I would have been quick to agree, this time I felt defensive of her.

"Well, I don't think that my father was good for Mai either. In fact, did you know that he dated her for five years without telling her that he had HIV? He put her life at risk. It's practically a miracle that she didn't get AIDS."

"No," Michelle stammered. "I didn't know that. But I don't believe it."

"Well, it's true . . . did you even know that my dad died from AIDS?"

"Yes . . . we heard that down in Florida," Alain cut in, pausing for a moment, "But I knew about your father's HIV years before."

"Years before?"

"Yes."

"He told you?"

"He confided in me. He needed someone to talk to."

"Really? Did he tell you *how* he contracted it?"

"He did, yes. I knew that too."

"Really? How was that? What did he tell you?"

"It's not really important for you to know? Is it?"

I tried to withstand his nerve long enough to get the information that I wanted.

"Actually, it is kind of important that I know. So if you know something, I'd like to hear it about it. It's really important for me to understand how this all happened to my family."

"Your dad was with a man. An experiment. Just once honestly. They didn't do much. It was just kissing, that kind of thing."

"That's it? Just kissing?" I said, rolling my eyes at him.

"Yes. It was with a Spanish man. His name slips my mind."

When it came to men Papa was particularly homophobic. His nephew Remy came from France to live with us when I was in middle school. When Remy moved to New York City a few years later, he came out as a gay man. While Papa adored Remy and literally called him "Junior," which now seems enormously ironic, he would never want to hear details about Junior's relationships with men, and would never legitimize Junior's identity.

"I don't want a faggot for a nephew," Papa said to him. I remember Junior telling me how painful it was not to have had his uncle's acceptance. Junior was not close to his own parents in France, and had desperately wanted my father's approval and affirmation about his identity, which Papa always refused to give him.

While it had passed through my mind that Papa could have contracted AIDS from a man, I'd always dismissed the possibility. Nothing about his behavior ever clued me in to this aspect of his identity. If I'd entertained the idea simply because gay male sex was a tremendous risk factor for the spread of HIV, I'd outruled it just as quickly. This was a facet of who he was that I would not have believed had there not been more than one firsthand witnesses, which is why I began speaking to other people that might know something.

CHAPTER FORTY-NINE

LA VIE HADN'T CHANGED much since Papa sold his share to his partner François in 1994 before he moved to Florida. The interior was practically the same: tables elegantly set, the straw ceiling, which mimicked the manger of Jesus's birthplace, the minibar where I'd drunk innumerable Shirly Temples, the coat room where as a girl I'd worked for Papa, handing out tickets and gently hanging coats for his patrons. Walking in there after all those years displaced me . . . Papa could have easily walked out of the kitchen with his white chef uniform on, and I could have easily just driven in from Long Island for dinner with some friends.

Hi, doll. Hi, girls. What can I get you? We have some specials tonight. The roasted rack of lamb, the mahimahi, salmon in mustard sauce. Whatever you'd like. . . .

Instead, François greeted me and found us a quiet table. He offered me some wine and showed me the menu, treating me to dinner. The cuisine had changed from Papa's Parisian cuisine to a southern French cuisine which had lighter sauces and a lighter feel.

"Can I ask you something?" François said. "Your grandmother told me on the phone that it was a brain tumor that your father died from. But was it AIDS?"

"Yes," I said. "It was. How did you know?"

"I heard rumors. In the restaurant world word travels

fast. People down in Florida who went to the funeral spoke to friends up here in New York. The word got around, but I wanted to be sure."

"I know Mai told a few people."

"Right."

"What do you know about my father's sexuality François? Please tell me the truth."

"Well, I knew of your father's bisexuality from the time we worked at Le Relais together. There were men he would get close to. Obviously this was something he tried to keep secretive, but in a restaurant culture word about things gets out, and he couldn't really keep it entirely hidden although I'm sure he'd have liked to. What I didn't realize about him before I went into business with him here at *La Vie* was just how much of a partyer he was. The way he abused drugs and alcohol. I just had no idea how serious his usage was."

"Alcohol I was aware of," I said.

"Cocaine," he said. "A lot of cocaine."

"What about heroin?"

"I don't think it was heroin, no."

"My dad knew that he was living with HIV," I said. "Since 1986. Did you have any idea about this?"

"No. No I didn't," François shook his head, in surprise. "But I have to tell you that puts into perspective why he was so adamant about the restaurant having a good life-insurance policy. He must have wanted to protect your mother and you kids in case he died while he was still an owner here which in the end didn't happen since sold his share and moved to Florida. I guess he lived much longer than he thought he might have."

"Do you think my mother knew that he was involved with men?"

"I doubt it very much. Did your cousin, Remy Junior, know that your dad was gay?"

"Junior never said he knew anything about it. No. Although he did tell me that he heard rumors about my dad doing coke. So you think my dad was gay?"

"He liked women too," François said.

"Do you know any of the men that my father was involved with? Where they are now? I met a man recently named Alain who said that dad was involved at one point with a Spanish man. Do you know if it was Luis, the chef from Argentina, that worked here, who died of AIDS when I was in high school?"

"I'm not sure. Luis was a heroin addict. I'm not sure if he was gay. But I don't know anyone else, no."

"I spoke to one other friend of my father's, a painter named Jacques.

"Yes. I remember Jacques very well," François said.

"Jacques told me that Luis was married."

"Did he know anything about your father and men?"

"He said that my dad used to ask him to go out to gay clubs with him. He had no interest in men, and he remembered very clearly telling my father that even if he did like men, he wouldn't have wanted to "die stupidly.""

"Hmm," François said. "That's interesting. So, it's a mystery about Luis, I guess."

"I'm not sure if he was the Spanish man whose name Alain could not remember."

"We may never know."

"Maybe not."

Afterthought

It's a strange thing to have thought your past was so different from what it was and to learn that the people who you thought you knew so well in some sense were strangers. When I first found out that my family members had known of Papa's HIV status for most of my childhood, I wondered a great deal about whether they should have told me and Luc sooner. The first instinct when finding out you have been deceived (even if you were deceived because of good intentions) is to wish that you weren't, that you had been told about the elephant standing in the room. When the shock wore off, I had more compassion for the decision that the adults made not to divulge the secret to young children. And while as an adult with a much deeper capacity to handle pain, I'd pick the truth any day over continually being lied to, I'm not sure they made the wrong decision to keep us protected from the information when we were younger and more vulnerable. Sometimes I imagine a parallel universe: I was ten and Luc was six. Mommy and Papa sat us down and explained to us that Papa had this deadly disease that people everywhere were dying from. We lived in fear that he would die. We cherished our moments with him, knowing that they could be some of the last but they were ridden with fear and sadness and longing. Mommy got tested and learned that she was also positive. Her doctors knew that she was exposed by her husband and treated her accordingly. When she got sick with Synovial Sarcoma, they knew that it was AIDS related. We had time to prepare for her death, but we simultaneously struggled through the knowledge that Papa didn't have much time. We lived constantly with the fear that we'd be orphans.

If we were told the truth, no doubt the suffering would have been insurmountable. But the trouble with being told a lie is that the truth affects you anyway. Even though you don't have the knowledge to think about the reality of what is going on, you still feel its effects. You can't see the elephant in the room, but you still feel what that elephant does. Even when a lie is told to protect you, you don't stay entirely protected.

So I struggle about which option would have been better . . . to have suffered with the truth or to have suffered with the lie. And I wonder what I'd do if faced with a similar dilemma. Would I be forthright with my own children or would I protect them to try to spare them from as much anguish as I could? Would I keep on nightlights?

I think about what contrasts with a soothing nightlight. Maybe it is a bright, glaring light. A light so bright and glaring that it causes nothing but pain. Or perhaps it is pitch-black darkness, completely terrifying.

It's equally strange to be the sole member of the family interested in bringing the truth to light. Every member of every family has a role or varied roles that they play and for whatever reason, I've staked out this particular role for myself in mine. I've pushed for my father's death from AIDS to be public and moreover pushed for the recognition from most of my family members that my parents's deaths were connected. It was hard to have a voice at first among the people I was closest to in the world because no one wanted to take what I was saying to heart.

Denial was such a pervasive way of life in my family, a silent language spoken, and I've thought a lot about how it's served different people in different ways.

With the denial that Mommy's cancer was AIDS related, Grandma and Grandpa were able to absolve themselves of deep and painful guilt. They knew they had encouraged her to stay in her marriage to my father and, if they were to really address to themselves that Papa gave her AIDS, they wouldn't have been able to live with themselves. Were they to admit in the 1980s when Mommy got sick that Papa could have infected her it would mean the breakdown of the family unit: they would have to stop loving him as a son-in-law, an integral member of their family, and they would have to watch their daughter's family unravel into chaos when she was at her most vulnerable. Through their denial, they were able to keep viewing Papa as a victim: a man who was HIV positive who had a wife dying from cancer. This narrative was convenient as it allowed for the family unit that they valued first and foremost to stay together, particularly during a trying time: the deathly illness of one of its members.

I'm uncertain whether Mommy's denial about her own HIV shortened or lengthened her life. One reason I am convinced that she did not make a conscious connection between my father's HIV status and her own cancer and blame him for her sickness is because of a letter I found that she wrote. It is dated December 19, 1990, which was my parents's sixteenth wedding anniversary, which fell just several months before she died in April of 1991.

Dear Remy,

Thank you for all the wonderful memories and for the love and support you have given me. You have shown me what true caring and love means, especially in times of adversity. Thank you for our two beautiful children and for keeping the marriage a lasting and enduring one. I love you and hope we can celebrate happier times together in future years. I am sorry for all the pain I have caused you. I wanted to give you much, much more, but I'll keep on trying.

Ilene.

I think her unwillingness to see Papa as responsible for what happened to her gave her the strength to go on living, the strength to continue being a mother for two small children. She did her very best to create a sense of normalcy for us and maybe if she hadn't denied the truth to herself she would have become lost in her own fear or rage or sadness and been less able to cope with the brutal challenges that life forced upon her. The strategy she used helped her to hold things together while I have to wonder how keeping her exposure to HIV hidden from her oncologists benefited her physical health. I also have to wonder whether being tested could have prevented so much of the suffering she went through. Perhaps her life could have been prolonged if she'd been under the care of a doctor who she was truthful with from much earlier on.

It served Papa well to deny that Mommy's death was related to him, obviously, because it exempted him from the responsibility of causing her death. I assume that on a conscious level he completely embraced the family narrative of her cancer arising from the complications of a childhood ski accident. Even if he suspected he played a role, it might have been easy to slip into denial about it since the people around him enabled that. As for what he told himself to justify what he did to Mai, I just can't know.

I don't think that he was in treatment for HIV. Even when the nature of AIDS changed in the eleven years that he lived with the virus and there were medications that were keeping people alive and healthy, I think he was still too scared to disclose anything to doctors and to risk being found out. He felt he had too much at stake: a business, children that could be affected negatively by the word getting out, numerous life insurance policies that might cut him off if they knew he was HIV positive.

Learning that his identity was more complex than I'd previously believed helped me to heal. It allowed me to contextualize what happened to my parents. I saw that my story was not just the story of AIDS devastating a family, which happens to so many people every day throughout the world in totally gruesome ways, but the story of men living on the down low and the insidious effects on their wives and families. The phenomenon of men living out their gay desires in secrecy calls into question the larger values of society, which enables this behavior and leads to insufferable consequences. In a world where having gay desire is demonized, the hiding of it is bound to also have hideous repercussions.

My anger subsided when I was able to link Papa's identity with my own. The fact that I was able to do something that he could not: live openly and freely as who I was gave me more compassion for his struggle. While I still don't know the extent of what his attraction to men was, I know enough to believe that from the early years of his marriage to Mommy he was struggling with a crucial secret. The secret that he struggled with was the same secret that I struggled with: the secret of having a need that society does not admire and furthermore vilifies. And while I don't condone his choices to lie or cheat, at least I can understand now what might have caused his behavior. The fear that everything around you will fall apart if you are to be yourself. It was oddly comforting to learn that he had been attracted to men. It gave me further conviction about who I was and it encouraged me to accept myself and to do what he had been unable to. I was his progeny and in a new generation, I was able to be true to myself, to be forthright and honest about something that he had to lie about, continually covering his tracks. Had he been honest about whom he was and what he was experiencing, he might have had the support of the gay male community in the 1980s when he got sick. From the conversations I've had with gay men who remember that time, as much suffering as there was, there was a strong sense of community: a place for people to share what they were enduring in the wake of the AIDS crisis.

Finale: 1995

Papa called me at college and asked me if I wanted to go on an impromptu trip with him to San Francisco. Every once in a while he got nostalgic for the place that he lived when he first moved to the States. He liked to show me the sights of where he and Mommy used to go together when they first fell in love.

We were driving together over the Golden Gate, after eating dinner in Sausalito. "Order whatever you want, doll," Papa had said. "Enjoy life while you have it."

There was a distracted look in his eyes as he drove; I knew that something was bothering him.

"What's wrong with you Papa?"

"Nothing . . . I'm just worried about business. The restaurant in Florida isn't doing well these days."

"It will get better," I said.

"You're right," he said. "I shouldn't worry. Things will get better."

"Right. Don't worry."

"Okay," he paused, his eyes wandering out to the bay, focusing back on our conversation.

"So are there any boys in your life?" he laughed.

I was quiet at first and then the bravery I needed crept up on me.

"I want to be with women," I said.

"Really?" he asked. He seemed curious. There was no trace of anger in his voice. All of my worrying for all those years that he would not accept me suddenly felt silly.

"Yeah. I want to find someone. A special woman."

"You will," he said with conviction. "And it's fine with me if you're with women."

"It is?"

"Yeah. Plus it's safer."

"Safer?"

"Yes."

"Oh . . ." I wasn't sure what he meant.

"I have no problem with it. Just be who you are, doll," he assured me. "I'll love you no matter what."

"Thank you," I said. "I appreciate that."

I watched the bay from the Golden Gate, captivated by the beauty of the water, of the colorful city on a hill where my parents found their fate, each other, of which my life was born.

"I've heard that so many gay men have AIDS here. A friend of mine from Cornell told me that so many people die here every year. Isn't that sad?"

He paused and nodded. "It is sad. It's very sad . . . you know, I know some people in New York who died from AIDS. You remember my old friend Luis, right?"

"Yes. Luis, the Argentinean chef. The one who you used to bring soup to when he got sick."

"Right," Papa laughed. "Luis was a great guy."

We parked the car and began window-shopping. Papa followed me into The Body Shop, so I could buy makeup. He was spoiling me again, and he told me to get whatever I wanted. At the checkout line, there was a sign for the sale of bracelets. They were sterling silver with elevated metal ribbons on their ends. I read on a sign that the proceeds from the sales went to AIDS research and care.

"Take one of those bracelets, doll," Papa said. "It's a good cause." He tightened it on my wrist for me when I took it out of the box, and told me not to lose it.